Soccer calling:
A Handbook for Youth Soccer coaches

BY DEAN CONWAY

**Library of Congress
Cataloging - in - Publication Data**

by Dean Conway
 Soccer Calling: A Handbook for Youth
 Soccer Coaches

ISBN No. 1-59164-097-0
Lib. of Congress Catalog No. 2005926725
© 2005

*Art Direction, Layout,
Proofing and Cover Design*
Bryan R. Beaver

Photos by
Front Cover: Jennifer Abelson
Back Cover: Daley Photography
Others: Richard Kentwell and
Robyn McNeil

Printed by
DATA REPRODUCTIONS
Auburn, Michigan

Reedswain Publishing
562 Ridge Road
Spring City, PA 19475
800.331.5191
www.reedswain.com
info@reedswain.com

Contents

Introduction

All over the world, people love soccer. They play the beautiful game, coach it, referee it, guide it as administrators, and follow it as passionate fans. Girls and boys, women and men from Stockholm, Soweto, Tokyo, and Mexico City play soccer, talk about it, read about it, and pull on jerseys and scarves and head for stadiums to watch it. It's one of a few universal phenomena on the planet. There's a game going on right now on a beach in Costa Rica, in a side street of Naples, on fields in Senegal and Bhutan.

Youth soccer has now become a genuine part of America's unique, fascinating, complex culture. As the game has become more and more popular, with so many kids now playing, the need for a large number of thoughtful and knowledgeable coaches has grown. This book is intended for coaches of U6 to U14 players, to provoke their thinking about their role in this sport, in our distinctive culture, and to offer some practical ideas for management and for organizing practices.

Whatever your involvement in soccer – thanks for all that you do for kids and for the game, and best wishes.

Dean Conway
January, 2005

I dedicate this book, gratefully, to my family.

Acknowledgements

I've been coaching soccer now for about 30 years; in that time I've been fortunate to have met many extraordinary teachers and coaches who have inspired me and stimulated my thinking about the game. This book is almost entirely derivative; I am indebted to countless colleagues and acquaintances for the ideas and notions here, and it would be virtually impossible to recognize all of them. The list runs from my own coaches when I played to my 'teammates' at the Massachusetts Youth Soccer Association to the bright conversationalists I've run into at many conventions over the years – to many other people. I feel particularly grateful to the coaches of the Dutch and Swedish Federations whom I have encountered. I would like to recognize three people in particular, though:

The late Bob McNulty, who taught the first coaching course I ever attended and showed me a wonderful example of who a coach should be.

Jape Shattuck: the way he thinks about soccer, humanity and education has always inspired me.

Bert van Lingen, the most astute soccer thinker I have ever encountered – for his generosity and inspiration over the years.

Warmup

This book is a collection of opinions, notions, cultural reflections, and practical suggestions. They all spring out of and are tied together by a few controlling ideas:

About soccer:

- Sports come out of local culture. In an observation on the state of the world, the Vatican once asserted that sports were "one of the nerve centers of contemporary culture." The culture that is the reference point for this book is the fast, competitive, ultra-organized, comparative, exciting, active, intense, impatient, turbo-charged, wonderful one of twenty-first century America.

  Many of the characteristics of our culture can inhibit, even work against, youth soccer. The organization, desire for control and predictability, competitive aura, and diligent commitment that characterize our culture do not create, necessarily, the best background for a fun-filled youth soccer experience. In the best case, adults focus on the children, hold themselves in the background, and turn the game, to the extent that it is possible, over to the kids. In the worst case, adults take the game away from the kids owing to a misplaced, compulsive desire to organize and an ego-driven competitive impulse.

- Soccer is a simple, free, unpredictable, fascinating game. It's not too much of a stretch to say that it is often "out of control", and it certainly often defies expectations. Some say that it is like moving chess. Only remotely: it goes too fast for truly calculated planning. Teams organize their midfields – but here comes Zidane, sprinting at them with the ball in front of him. Now what?! Your back line is forewarned – but here comes Ronaldinho, with a little smile on his face and the ball, tantalizingly, between his feet. Now what?! A center back heads the ball away from his own goal – but it hits an opponent in the side of the head and bounces into the goal. Anything can happen!

We're engaged in a powerful, enthralling world-wide cultural force: this is one of the only activities that people everywhere engage in. Let's tap into that power and let the attraction of the ball and the mystical fascination of the game work their magic.

About children:

- Every child is different from every other child, and children change every day.

- The most important aspect of soccer for young players is technique. Then the players must learn how to use the skills, the tools – to solve tactical problems, which always involve teammates and opponents and space and which always occur in momentary, fleeting, unpredictable circumstances. The players must learn how to dominate the moment. So there are two big challenges for a player: to play well with the ball and to play well with teammates.

- Youth soccer practices should be first and foremost FUN. Tough and challenging, sure, as the years go by. But from the first to the last, FUN. They should also be about freedom, imagination, discovery, trial and error, respect, fair play, creativity, perception and decisiveness.

- Youth soccer practices and games should be much more about youth, much less about adults. More youthful spirit, less 'commitment'; more "See what you can do.", less "Do what I told you."; more the simplicity and joy and constant renewal of childhood and less our adult agenda: more play, less work.

- There is always a tension in youth soccer between regard for the present and regard for the future. This can be a subtle and complex issue, and it can detract from the enjoyment of the children and their parents and from the effectiveness of the coach. In simplest terms, the kids up to about the age of eight have little regard for the future: they act almost entirely in the here and now: soccer is just movement, scoring, chasing, fun. Kids older than seven or eight still play mainly for fun and enjoyment, and if they consider the future, their thinking is mostly in the realm of daydreaming, imagining nice outcomes, trying to play like the big stars.

  - Parents are well advised to concentrate more on the present, less on the future. Too many of them are pre-occupied with what soccer will lead to: making a big club, getting a scholarship. What will be, will be. A positive course is to cheer and support your child, be aware of and take advantage of sound opportunities, and take your cue from your child's desires and hopes.

  - Coaches are well advised to generate as much enthusiasm, sound teaching, and fun as possible; to keep everything in patient, long-term perspective; and to acknowledge that they should and must think much more about the future than their players do.

About adults:

- One of our biggest challenges as leaders or teachers or coaches of soccer teams in this culture where dynamism, diligent work habits, and productivity are so highly valued, will be to figure out how to do as little as possible at practices and in games. This is one of the many ironies of youth soccer.

- We're engaged in helping kids to become better soccer players, of course. We're also engaged in helping them to become strong, upright, positive human beings. Of every 100 kids who play U6 to U14 youth soccer, only a very few will be playing organized, formal soccer past high school – although one hopes that they're all playing pickup soccer for a long time to come. So we must ask ourselves what these kids are going to derive from their involvement in youth soccer. If the answer is: plenty of enjoyment and satisfaction from playing, good health and a life-long commitment to fitness, lots of friends, a positive outlook and strong sense of fairness, and a more receptive and patient approach to life, then we've done well!

• In all our words and actions among the kids: positive, not negative; encouraging, not critical.

• We should always be concerned most with the heart, the spirit, the artistic side – of the kids and the game.

Chapter One

11 Important Traits for Youth Soccer Coaches

Coaching youth soccer is a social, emotional, personal activity, so it makes sense to consider first of all the human characteristics that are vital for an enjoyable and successful experience as a coach. Especially when dealing with young kids, the character and qualities of a coach are extremely important.

Enjoyable and effective coaching relies on an individual's ability to blend positive character traits and strong organizational abilities, and, with more experienced players, expertise in the sport in question. For coaches of the youngest soccer players – those in the U6 and U8 group – personal qualities are paramount. As a matter of fact, the adults who guide those youngest players should perhaps not even be called "coaches"; in Norway, for example, they are called "activity leaders". In this book the word "coach" will be used freely, but it might make more sense if the adult in question was called, at U6 and U8 level, an "activity leader", at U10 and U12 level a "soccer teacher", and at U14 and after that as a "coach".

The youngest kids just need someone to introduce the game to them in a patient, kind, understated way. At the next stage – U10 and U12 – coaches must have solid organizational abilities and should know about soccer, but personal character traits are still vitally important. Even when players get to the U14 or U16 level and are more self-reliant, resilient, and resourceful, the way that a coach acts and speaks is central.

Youth soccer coaches should consider themselves first of all as teachers and sources of inspiration and encouragement – not as "motivators" trying to build a winning team or as recruiters. Parents should expect the same sort of mature, sensitive approaches and attitudes from coaches as they do from their children's teachers. It's not reasonable for parents to expect that their child's youth soccer coach, who is most likely a volunteer, will necessarily be trained in coaching methodology and know a lot about the game. They should be assured, though, that the coach is a fine model of adulthood.

From a coach's point of view, too, maximizing certain traits will make everything smoother and more enjoyable. People with rigid approaches or short tempers, or those who are hyper-competitive or impatient are probably going to have a tough time leading a group of young athletes; it's best for them to moderate those behaviors and to maximize other, more positive traits.

Here are eleven personality traits worth cultivating:

1. Enthusiasm

Good activity leaders and coaches exude energy and high spirits and enthusiasm. Their positive spirit is visible – in their alertness, their gestures, and their body language. Kids are intuitive: they feel us with a lot more sensitivity and acuity than we sometimes imagine. If we're smiling and upbeat, our voices are inflected, and our expressions all positive, that's a huge contribution to a practice environment or a game day.

2. Patience

A wonderful coach, Zissis Papanikolaou, of the Greek club Piraeus, once said, "The most difficult thing for a coach is to manage frustration." What an insight! Coaching youth soccer is fun and satisfying, but it can also be quite frustrating. The practice field is still soggy, the referee just missed another obvious handball in their penalty area, so many kids look unfocused again tonight....

And there's more! One of the ironies of this whole activity is that many leaders or coaches start coaching out of the goodness of their hearts: they don't know much about soccer, but they want to help. Then almost immediately they're put under pressure – as often by the parents as by the players – to be or at least to look authoritative and influential, which often means to win games.

In fact, there is a long list of potentially frustrating elements. An easy way to summarize the situation is to say that each practice and each game will present you, in your role as coach, with a constant stream of challenges and of mistakes. And some of these mistakes will be made by kids who don't seem to care or who wouldn't make them if you just... well... yelled at them sooner, or louder.

These frustrations are all the more difficult for people to accept because in their professional lives, things are so different. At work they expect, as they should, concentration, responsiveness, and consistency from those around them. Now at practice, kids are daydreaming, looking unconvinced after that tactical lecture, and making one technical mistake after another. At work, we like to see projects through to the end; here we're with the kids only for a little while, and we won't see the "finished product" ninety-five per cent of the time. At our jobs we like things to be predictable and people to be accountable; here we're dealing with a tremendously unpredictable game with kids who, for the most part, just want to have some fun (which is, of course, exactly why they should be playing!).

You and your players will have a much more enjoyable time, and your leading or coaching will be much more effective if you accept several realities:

- Kids are kids, not small adults. They may seem, or in fact be, self-possessed, sophisticated, and savvy, even precocious, but an eight year old is an eight year old, and a twelve year old is a twelve year old. That means that their perceptions are limited (and that has nothing to do with their intelligence); they have shorter and narrower attention spans than we might like. They can be moody, flighty, dreamy, inconsistent, lethargic, provocative (like us!) and not even notice (like us!).

- Most of what we are involved with here is out of our control: the way they play, the lapses and errors that frustrate them too: the wind, field, opponent, referee. We should control what we can, like the time and space of practice activities and our own demeanor on game days, and be patient about the rest.

- There is nothing wrong with a measured word once in a while to get the attention of U12 or U14 players and get them into the game.

- Of course, there are some things you should not be patient with: unkindness to another player, disruptive behavior or disrespect of an opponent, for example.

- There is another particular aspect of leading or coaching that tries the patience of almost all coaches, and the more that we as coaches are alert to and accepting of this situation, the better. That is: learning soccer (and just about everything else) takes a great deal of time. Often, coaches demonstrate a technique or explain a tactical situation and then their players begin to practice or begin to play in a game. The coach may then look out on the field and think, "It's as if I never showed them this – or never explained that!"

Patience! Becoming a skillful, intelligent player takes time, practice, repetition and trial and error. This is not to advocate complacency or to discourage reasonable challenges to the players; it is only to state that we must allow sufficient time for learning to occur – and that learning is usually measured in years, not months or weeks.

The more patient and accepting you are, the more relaxed the players are bound to be: they'll see the field better and be more inclined to try new techniques. The great South African player Steven Pienaar was asked how he had managed, at just 21, to become a star at the big Amsterdam club Ajax and to make the South African national team. He replied that, besides always training hard, he had been given freedom to express himself.

The need for patience in a youth soccer coach can not be overstated. Coaching is enjoyable and fulfilling, for sure, but

there are going to be consistent frustrations and even provoca-
tions: a baffling range of abilities and levels of motivation among
the 10 players on your team, 11 year old wise guys, a know-it-all
parent, a loss to a team that just plays kick and run, etc., etc.
The list goes on and on. **Stay cool! Enjoy everything!**

3. Humor

The world of childhood, and of adulthood, too, for that
matter, should be characterized by joy and open-mindedness,
innocence, discovery, and FUN. In fact, the world of children is
increasingly serious. Adult concerns and pressures seem to
intrude more and more because of the pace of life, the media,
the rush to grow up. The world of youth sports, which should be
a haven of joy and exhilaration and enchantment, can feel, these
days, very serious. Humor can help: it lightens the atmosphere,
brings people together and decreases anxiety. It promotes
acceptance of mistakes: athletes have to be able to laugh at
themselves and the sometimes weird, random bounces of the
ball. The word "humor" here is certainly to be distinguished from
'goofiness': underlying respect for the wonderful quality of soccer
and for all the people involved must prevail. It is also, of course,
to be distinguished from sarcasm, which has a bite to it and is in
no way child-like.

Humor can have another positive impact on the kids.
They're involved in soccer for many reasons, the primary one
being that it is, simply, fun. They're also intuitively and subconsciously absorbing ideas about life all the time, as they interact
with their coaches at practices and games. In some cases, they
observe a world where there's clearly, in their child-like perceptions, too much seriousness and tension and anxiety. On the
other hand, they sometimes observe an environment where
things are balanced and light-hearted and smiles are prevalent.
That's a nice world view for them, for the moment.

4. Organization and clarity

Some people seem to have a knack for being organized:
they're punctual and relaxed; they never seem rushed. There is

purpose in their actions, but they don't get compulsive. They speak clearly and coherently; they are linear thinkers. Part of this gift is intuitive, part the result of education, part the result of self-willed mental training – that is, practice.

Activity leaders and coaches should be organized and clear:

- Take the time to make a simple plan before each practice. Try to develop a realistic sense of how much you can accomplish. When in doubt, plan less than you think you should: most people try to do too much.

- Wear a watch and look at it often.

- Speak as little as possible. This is a tough objective! Most coaches, once they start to talk, have a hard time stopping. And if you're only seeing the kids once or twice a week, there is often a mysterious, sub-conscious force pushing you along saying, "Come on, talk more!" as some sort of validation for your presence. Or maybe you just like to talk! Remember: as important as what you have to say may be, and as much affection as the players feel for you, they never come to practice to listen to a coach talk. They come for one reason, so we should try to let them do that as much as possible. It takes great self-discipline to speak less, too; a brief message is always better on a soccer field.

5. Sincerity

All your words and actions among the players, at practices and games, and among the parents, should be genuine. We should always ask for realness and honesty from our players, and ourselves. Players from their earliest days should not evade, they should acknowledge mistakes, they should support teammates who make unfortunate errors (missing open goals, letting an easy shot roll through their legs when they're playing goalkeeper, etc.). A soccer field is a wonderful place to learn to be wholehearted and responsible.

14

One of the many challenges coaches face is the issue of how occasionally to temper sincerity with discretion, how to speak truthfully but diplomatically. We should always aim to be direct and truthful, but sensitive. Kids are observant and intuitive, and they literally and figuratively 'know the score'. If we gloss over real mistakes by calling them "unlucky", the kids are not served well. If, on the other hand, we dwell on the mistake or blame anyone, they will, understandably, become discouraged.

There are often clear examples of sincerity – or lack of sincerity – on the field during high level games, which is another good reason for our players to watch those games in person or on television. Sometimes when a player on the opposing team has been injured, the team in possession will knock the ball out of bounds, instead of playing on with a momentary advantage. When that player has received treatment or been substituted, the team now in possession will throw the ball back to the team originally in possession on the ensuing throw-in. That's good. On the other hand, players will sometimes 'dive' in the penalty area, pretending to be fouled, trying to bait the referee into making a call. That's bad – and draws deserved scorn from the other team. The fact that the referee can now give that insincere player a yellow card is a positive development in the evolution of the laws of the game.

Fair play, honest efforts, a genuine approach: that's soccer!

6. Humility and restraint

Youth soccer is for the kids – it's not really 'for' us or 'about' us. Any concerns that we have for building up our own reputation through our involvement in the game are questionable at best. We can't go wrong if we constantly apply the excellent motto of the Swedish Soccer Federation: Players at the center. We should win gracefully and lose graciously and hope that we can convince our players to do that, too.

During games we should try to be as quiet as possible. Our impulses or our anxiety may lead us to call out to our players, to make suggestions, even to give orders or script the action.

We should restrain ourselves: let the players play, explore, discover, make mistakes, figure things out, work through problems. It's their game.

Recently, the following remarks were printed in a column in The New York Times:

> "As parents, we have all seen our children in pressure-packed situations, surrounded by ultracompetitive coaches. This merely takes the joy out of the game for the kids, and, ultimately, turns them off from whatever sport they are playing.
> During games, parents and coaches can be over the top with their support, cheering wildly whenever anything positive occurs. But when the action turns negative for their child or team, the parents grow silent. In my view, these actions send very negative messages to the kids.
> As a parent, I understand how extremely difficult it is to sit quietly as your child competes. But teaching and correcting should not take place during the game. This is a time to let the kids compete the best they can without feedback. The time for teaching is the next day or two days later, when the emotion from the game is gone and the children are more open to learning."

That's Cal Ripken, Jr., speaking about youth baseball.

7. Affection

In everything we do, affection for our players should be obvious. Our concern for them as developing human beings, not just as soccer players, is vital: we should always try to empathize with them, see as they see, hear as they hear. As difficult as it is sometimes, we should accept their limitations and mistakes with perspective and humor, never with anger or blameful criticism.

It is unfortunate that in the current atmosphere, with revelations of child abuse pervading the media, people have to think twice about showing affection for children. It's good to be spontaneous and demonstrative, but coaches should also be aware of themselves and be careful about any physical gestures – even a kind one like a hug - that they make.

8. Empathy and imagination

It is vital that as coaches we try occasionally to walk in our players' shoes: to try to imagine what they are seeing and hearing, and how they are feeling. Players want to feel that we understand them, that we like and appreciate them, that we're on their side.

Remembering our own childhood and our athletic adventures and misadventures can help us to shape our coaching personality, too. Most of us can remember incidents and situations that were happy and satisfying, that made us proud. We can also remember incidents and situations that were embarrassing or upsetting. Some of these memories probably include coaches who inspired us, taught us a lot, created a wonderful environment for us; other memories may include coaches who were rather harsh or critical or impatient. Going back in time imaginatively can provide us with lots of guidance as to what kind of coach we want to be.

A lively imagination can also animate our coaching by suggesting how we can change practice activities, play people in different positions, motivate our team. An imaginative approach can also help us to apply what we know about other sports (and many youth soccer coaches know plenty about other sports!). There are many tactical analogies between basketball and soccer, and technical similarities between hitting a tennis ball or a golf ball and striking a soccer ball, for example. We should encourage imagination in our players, too – because they're playing a game with a fabulous range of possibilities and opportunities. Every time one player dribbles forcefully at a defender, every time two players attack a lone defender, at every set play: who's to say what will happen?

9. Curiosity

Soccer coaches should be eager to learn and should always be asking questions- of their players, their colleagues, and themselves.

Soccer is a game for dynamic thinkers, problem solvers, those with lively minds. We coaches should be stimulating the kids and challenging them from their earliest days as players: asking them questions as opposed to constantly making statements, provoking their own curiosities. It is probable that the more we tell them what to do, the less curious they will become. We want to develop teams of <u>thinkers</u> as well as teams of athletes, fighters and artists. All too often, kids at the U14, U16, or U18 stages, when their techniques are stable and their fitness levels high, do not have the kinds of lively, alert minds they should. They have – more or less – the skills they need, and they're fast and strong, but their imaginations and will power and creative thrust all seem underdeveloped. Could that be because all their lives one coach after another has told them what to do, as opposed to questioning and stimulating and provoking them?

The Socratic method can be just as effective on the soccer field as it is in a classroom, too: we coaches should probe and question and 'open things up' and then see what kinds of answers and solutions come forth from the players. If we can set up an environment where we are constantly asking good, clear questions and the kids are energetically and openly answering or offering ideas: that's teamwork!

We should be reflecting and asking ourselves questions all the time, too. How can I give more confidence to Alice? Where can I find a couple more good shooting games? Should we play with three or four in the back line? I should check with Ron soon. I wonder what he's been reading. Of course, the central question is: How can I become a better coach?

10. Open-mindedness

Over the years, soccer maintains its spontaneous, unpredictable, free-flowing essence, but certain elements of the game change in subtle ways. There are nice examples of technical novelty, like Johan Cruyff's famous turn, or passes with the chest, or clever dribbling moves. Tactically, the game is a big pot of opinions: 4 – 4 – 2 or 4 – 3 – 3 or ? At 1 – 0, go for another goal or hang on? Press hard from the start or sit back? And there are always new ideas about psychology and in the realm of fitness: motivational ideas, a 'better' way to stretch, a new insight about nutrition or speed work. So it's good to be open-minded, receptive to new thinking, new possibilities.

A parent may suggest something, a fellow coach may mention an article she just read, a clinician may challenge your thinking in a seminar you've attended: those are all worth thinking about. You may or may not end up coming to a different conclusion, but it's good to get into the habit of pausing and reflecting, looking at the other side. It's distressing to run into coaches who, for one reason or another (lack of patience, defensiveness, a stubborn nature, etc.), are not open-minded, who reject new ideas without a second thought.

It is particularly important to be open-minded with your players. A central truth about youth soccer coaching is that you never know how kids are going to develop. The kid who is a hot striker at 11 may be, at 15, playing rhythm guitar in a band and be done with soccer. That excellent, aspiring goalkeeper at 13 may end up playing only basketball in high school. On the other hand, that clever U14 center half, whose coach raves about her, was, as you remember her, a mediocre, rather uncommitted player when she played on your U10 team. But you encouraged her, stuck with her, paid as much attention to her as to the other 'better' (at that moment!) players – and look at her now!

11. Friendliness

Just as youth soccer coaches should be kind and affectionate with their players, they should be friendly toward everyone else they encounter: parents, referees, opposing coaches.

It is especially desirable to establish friendly relations with parents: they are important to you, and you are important to them. By virtue of your position as leader or coach, you are now a prominent influence on their child, like a teacher at their school, or a relative. You'll help their child to develop, and you'll most likely end up educating the parents, at least indirectly, about soccer and athletics. You may confirm their thinking about their child, or, on the other hand, you may offer some fresh insights into their child's personality. Sometimes kids' true personalities are rather subdued or muted in the house or at school, but they 'come out' while the kids are playing sports. Sometimes you may tell parents how dynamic their daughter is, what a thoughtful problem solver their son is, how kind and positively influential their daughter is; those messages are happily received.

However, sometimes you have to address more difficult, awkward issues: disrespect, bad language, divisive or mean behavior. In that case, parents may react with, "My little Edgar? He's such an angel!" Or they may say, "Yes, well, he's ripping it up at home and at school, too." Whether or not your perceptions are the same, if you have friendly relations with the parents, it will be easier to build trust and to deal with those kinds of situations positively and effectively.

An amiable presence among referees and opposing coaches is positive, too: it's a sign of your good intentions and respect for the game. Anxiety or arrogance or the kind of edgy competitiveness that borders on hostility have no place in youth soccer.

It is fantastic to watch soccer at the highest level, when national teams compete, and to see the artistry and fighting power and tactical savvy. It's also wonderful to watch the moments right after those games when the players come together to wish one another well, hug one another, shake hands, exchange shirts. Even after the toughest games, it seems that the prevailing emotions are mutual respect and <u>friendliness</u>.

Chapter Two

11 Suggestions to Enhance Your Own Development

If you are among the great majority of youth soccer coaches, you are involved as a volunteer, and you're coaching as an avocation. A small minority of you are being paid to coach.

In either case, it is vital that you strive to keep learning and advancing. The more you know and the more you feel in command of your craft, the more enjoyable and rewarding coaching will be for you. The game is simple and straightforward, but it does evolve constantly, and you should resolve to stay up-to-date. Think about comparing a world atlas from 2004 to one published in 1970. Certainly the kids are getting better all the time – they're playing more soccer, watching games, thanks to the continually expanding offerings on television, attending camps and clinics, and, where it is available, going to watch professional matches. Even advertisements on television are stimulating and inspiring for kids. They're getting to be quite good players earlier and earlier, and we coaches have to try to stay ahead of them.

The time you have available to cultivate your coaching, the amount of money you can spend, your motivation: these factors are all personal and individual. It would be helpful, as you begin coaching, to take a few moments to consider how to plan your own education. Thinking about your own development is analogous to planning a practice session, in that there's never enough time. What you can't do immediately will have to wait. What should you do right away, what are realistic goals for this year, what about two or three years from now (assuming that, as I hope, you're committed to coaching for at least a few years)?

Here are 11 general ideas as you consider how to advance:

1. Devote one day – or weekend – a year to coach education

If you're just starting out, perhaps you could take a state level F Course or attend a one day clinic at a local college, or go to some coaching sessions at your state's youth soccer association's symposium. State level coaching courses are beneficial: they help you learn to organize and prioritize, they expose you to a lot of new ideas, methods, and resources, and they enable you to meet inspiring colleagues – the instructor and fellow coaches. You can generally find out about coach education offerings on your state association's website or by calling their office.

Let's say that you've just picked up a U8 team: your daughter is going to be on the team, and although you never played soccer, you're athletic and interested, so you volunteered. You're thinking vaguely – Well, I'll do this for three or four, maybe five years. Then she'll be through the U12 stage and will need somebody who knows more about soccer. So you make this (hypothetical) plan:

- This year, I'll take the one day F Course or an age specific youth module or go to the winter clinic that the local college always offers.
- Year two: an E Course or another youth module.
- Year three: that goalkeeper clinic that the high school coach offers in August.
- Year four: a D Course.
- Year five: a full day of sessions at the state's annual workshop.

If every youth coach devoted just one day a year to education, it would make a profound difference in the level of coaching we could collectively offer to the kids.

2. Go to good soccer games

Attending a high level soccer game – that is, a college or professional game – is enjoyable and edifying. And by going to the game, you're sustaining the sport as inspiration and entertainment. The proximity of the action, the 'feel' of the atmosphere, and the emotional immediacy are all stimulating. The fact that you can take in far more visually than you can on television is vitally important. You can watch how players away from the ball move; for example, how the goalkeeper and the back line players of one team position themselves with the ball at the other end of the field, or how all the players move on set plays. You can also watch the referee and her or his assistants, or the coaches, or the substitutes who are warming up.

So much the better if you go with someone who knows a lot about soccer. They can point things out to you, or the two of you can share ideas and opinions.

Soccer games can be as much for conversation as for enjoyment and analysis. During the first half, you and your friend can focus on various elements: he's watching the home team's attacking, you're watching their defending. At half time, you compare insights and talk about what you would be saying to the team if you were the coach. Then in the second half, you talk about books you're reading, recent movies, your families, natural law.

3. Join soccer organizations

There are many dynamic organizations dedicated to promoting soccer, educating coaches, and expanding the culture of the game. They provide resources like magazines, conventions, coaching courses, and gear. Involvement with them is a great way to stay on top of recent developments, maintain contact with other coaches, and continue your education.

The US Coaches Organization
United States Soccer Federation
1801 South Prairie Avenue
Chicago, IL. 60616
Phone: 312 808-1300
www.us-soccer.com

United States Youth Soccer Association
899 Presidential Drive
Suite 117
Richardson, TX. 75081
Phone: 800 4SOCCER
www.youthsoccer.org

National Soccer Coaches Association of America
6700 Squibb Road
Suite 215
Mission, KS. 66202
Phone: 800 458-0678
www.nscaa.com

American Youth Soccer Organization
12501 South Isis Avenue
Hawthorne, CA. 90250
Phone: 800 USA – AYSO
www.soccer.org

4. Subscribe to Success in Soccer

This is the best, most sophisticated coaching periodical
on the market. Every other month this magazine offers a comprehensive blend of articles for young players, 'middle' players, high
level amateurs, and professionals, from around the world.
The Success in Soccer company also offers excellent
coaching books and a first-rate series of videos.
Success in Soccer
PO Box 92046
Albuquerque, N.M. 87199
Phone: 888 828-4263
www.successinsoccer.com

5. Subscribe to <u>World Soccer</u>

The best soccer news periodical in the world: monthly reports that are thorough, measured, and professional. Their coverage of big events, like the World Cup or the Champions League tournament, is unparalleled. Superb photographs, too. If you want to pick up historical perspectives and learn about the culture of the modern game, <u>World Soccer</u> is indispensable. The writers and editors are thoroughly professional, and they transmit a dignified regard for all that is best and most desirable about soccer.

<u>World Soccer</u> also features occasional special features about one aspect of soccer or another; there was recently a superb report about youth development, filled with great insights and information.

The only criticism here: not enough (hardly anything) about the women's game.

6. Play!

If you have background in soccer, you know how wonderful it is to play. If you're just discovering the game, having come to it through coaching, you probably already know how enjoyable it is to play. The constant flow, the all-action quality, emotional engagement, physical challenge, and intellectual challenge of soccer are all exhilarating.

Playing soccer will enhance your fitness and health, provide a nice social occasion, and offer you a 'playful' outlet in your otherwise business-like schedule.

Playing also provides clear benefits in your role as a coach. It will remind you – or teach you – how unpredictable, random, and frustrating soccer can be, how complex it is tactically (in spite of its simplicity), and how refined it is technically. Playing the game will bring you closer the your players' emotional states and add some immediacy to any suggestions or guidelines you may offer to the parents of your players. If you play even occasionally you'll be better able to demonstrate ball skills to your players, too.

Getting out and playing may have another psychological benefit for some coaches, too. By giving them a competitive outlet of their own, it may make it easier for them to detach themselves emotionally from the competitive element of the games they're coaching – and easier to concentrate during those games on teaching and leading.

7. Take a referee's course and referee

If you have not played soccer, it is not reasonable to expect you to know the rules of the game. Even people who have played the game for a long time generally haven't paid much attention to the formal rules: they've just played.

The rules of soccer are designed to ensure that the game is fair and sporting and played in the proper spirit. They are logical, consistent, and intuitive. You can learn them simply by reading the rule book and by watching games carefully.

Another way to learn the rules is to take a referee's course. That's a positive route: you'll also be exposed to interpretations of the rules and techniques of game management. You'll meet aspiring referees and veteran referees and be able to talk with them about their concerns and opinions.

Once you feel confident that you know the rules, try to referee in some way. If you have the time and the inclination, refereeing competitive league games is satisfying, helpful, and edifying.

If your involvement in the game is in coaching your team, make it a point to referee during the end-of-practice scrimmage from time to time. Spending an occasional 20 to 30 minutes refereeing your split squad's practice game will be very enlightening. You'll get a distinct feel for the combativeness - or passivity - of your players, their assertiveness and strength, and you'll feel and gain a keen sense of the communication going on during their play.

Just as important, you'll understand how tough it is to referee. You may be surprised at the speed with which situations force themselves upon you. Handball or not? Foul or not? Offside or not? Come on, quick, make up your mind!

You'll see that referees must master the four components of soccer: technique, tactics, fitness, and mentality – just as players must. Referees must learn to run efficiently, backpedal, shuffle; they have to master the whistle so that it gives messages. Like a player, the more they can anticipate the action and position themselves effectively, the better. And if you begin to referee, you'll see the fine line that separates a tough challenge from a foul and the line that separates a foul from a yellow card, and you'll <u>feel</u> how fast you must decide where those lines are. Referees have to be super-fit; they can't take a break to catch their breath; mentally, too, they must stay in the game every moment, concentrate, be decisive, put mistakes behind them.

If all coaches would expose themselves to refereeing at least to the extent that they 'reffed' their team's scrimmages from time to time, they would develop empathy for referees, and the game would be better off. Referees are crucial to soccer, but they have a literally thankless job. Youth coaches should approach every game as a collaboration of players, coaches, and referees. Novice referees, like players and coaches, need time to develop. If beginners are discouraged and demoralized by constant criticism and hostility at games, and they stop refereeing, we're in trouble.

There is a movement in some youth soccer environments to keep coaches and referees apart, to stop all interactions among them. If that protects a young ref from abuse or harsh criticism or antagonism from the sidelines during a game, fine. But it may also constrict learning opportunities. If we could figure out a way to have knowledgeable, objective, experienced coaches (that should be all of us after a couple of years in the game!) get together with a young referee right after a game or shortly after a game, it could be quite helpful. The bottom line is: youth coaches should be dedicated to educating everyone they encounter: players, parents, colleagues, and referees, too. Youth soccer is about education.

8. Watch videos and read

An efficient and convenient way to improve your coaching is to watch videos or read about soccer from time to time. Depending on the amount of time you can dedicate to the game, you can make an objective: perhaps reading a book every year, or three books a year; watching a new video every year, or two videos every season. Reading an article about youth goalkeeping in <u>Success in Soccer</u> magazine, watching 20 minutes of the <u>Individual Attacking</u> tape from the International Tactics series, or making your way through <u>Coaching the Team</u>, by Tony Waiters, are wonderful, time-efficient ways to advance as a coach.

Watching videos and reading stimulate your thinking, make you more resourceful, and help keep you up to date.

9. Read about and learn about kids

In the world of youth soccer, our point of departure should be the kids, not the soccer. Central to everything we do should be the overall development of every child we encounter.

Most youth leaders or coaches get involved in soccer because their kids are now playing. Whether or not our children are involved, most of us do not have experience in childhood development, unless we are teachers or doctors. The world of children is fascinating, wonderful and often a little mysterious: it is good to learn as much about it as we can. The more we know about the way kids grow – physically, emotionally, psychologically, cognitively – the better.

Seek out, from your pediatrician or your local bookstore, good books about childhood development. Read the experts, people like Howard Gardner and Mel Levine and Carol Gilligan. Pick up <u>The New York Times</u> on Tuesdays and look at the

"Science Times" section. Exchange articles with other coaches, talk with your players' parents, watch for lectures or presentations at your local community college or community center.

Your involvement in soccer may spin off some very intriguing insights into your own children or those of your team.

10. Learn about nutrition and health and the prevention and care of injuries

There is no need to become an expert here – but it's helpful to be a voice of common sense, and, of course, we must always be responsible.

Many kids don't think about what they should eat or drink before, during, and after practices and games. We should help them learn, especially about hydration and drinking a sufficient amount of water or sports drink. The players should drink a good amount of water before practice or a game, they should have sufficient water during breaks, depending on climate and season, and they should begin re-hydrating as soon as a practice or game is over.

Two fine, comprehensive sources of information about nutrition are Nancy Clark's Sports Nutrition Guidebook and Nutrition for Soccer Players, by Enrico Arcelli.

All leaders and coaches should take a first aid course and a CPR course and should learn all that they can about how to prevent and care for injuries, especially the common soccer ones like contusions, ankle sprains, and muscle pulls (strains).

11. Watch good coaches at a practice

Seeing a great athlete play is inspirational and gratifying; watching a great coach lead a practice session is inspirational and gratifying, too.

Call a local college, semi-pro, or pro coach or talk with an experienced coaching colleague who has an excellent reputation:

ask them if you can drop in to a practice as an observer. Then watch the coach carefully: her organization, the way she begins, makes transitions, corrects, asks questions, paces activities, changes coaching position. How is her body language, her choice of words, her volume and inflection when she speaks?

One good reason to attend seminars and conventions is the opportunity to watch lots of excellent coaches in a concentrated period of time.

Chapter Three

Ideas to Pass on to Parents

Our primary function as youth soccer coaches is to coach soccer: to inspire, help, and teach the kids on our team. Of course, we can also help out with other elements of the game in our town or club: administration or refereeing, building up our library or ordering gear.

Another vital function for us is to teach the parents of our players about soccer and youth development and to help them to understand the world of youth soccer. That is sometimes more difficult than it should be. Parents may have misconceptions or misunderstandings or fantasies.

We live in a fast-paced, competitive, comparative culture: people want it now, they want to look good, to win, not to miss out on anything or to get left behind. It is natural and completely understandable for parents to be most focused on and concerned about their own child or children, but some become so anxious about and absorbed in their child that their attention is counter-productive. They may reflexively or irrationally think that, for youth soccer players, more and sooner are better. Or they may want their child to succeed because they were successful ath-letes - or because they were not successful athletes. There are many reasons why communication and understanding between parent and coach could be difficult.

In the happiest situation, the parents of your players are patient, calm, open-minded, receptive, and deferential. They are enthusiastic, but they keep things in perspective; they are active and alert, but they stay in the background; and they accept your decisions and leadership style. Their relationship to you is essentially the same as it is with any of their child's teachers; they consider you one more respected partner in their child's overall development. It is enjoyable to see them at practices and games: whatever you may have to say to them about their child, or they to you, conversation is positive and constructive. And even if you hardly ever see them, things are fine: they conform to all the team guidelines, their child is secure, and relations are friendly all around.

On the other hand, parents can be tough: edgy, anxious, even overbearing. They may become overcome with emotion at games, they may model questionable behavior, they may challenge you undiplomatically, or simply, because of some dissatisfaction, make your position far less pleasant than it should be.

Often, the parents of the players on your team reflect the composition of the team itself: there are some extraordinary ones, some who challenge your resource and patience, and many 'average, regular' ones in the middle. Whatever the composition of the parent group, we should try to be positive, dignified, friendly, and helpful. It is important to educate parents about the game, player development, the rules and soccer culture.

A brief, mandatory pre-season meeting for the parents is essential. "Every household should be represented." You can ask them to come 30 minutes early to the first practice and talk to them while the kids play 4 v 4 or have dessert one evening at your house before the season – whatever is convenient. If it is the very first meeting, you can introduce yourself, give them an idea of your background, and talk to them about logistical details: practice site and time, gear, etc.

You can also begin to talk philosophy with them, but that conversation should continue as the season or the seasons or the years go by. It is a good idea to have a meeting at the beginning of every season, for reminders and updates: as the kids grow, your priorities and approaches will most likely change. And, of course, the parents should feel free to call you any time.

Here are eleven ideas that are helpful to pass on to parents:

1. Youth soccer should be about FUN and learning.

The most important objective for youth soccer players is to have fun. The fact that playing soccer is fun is what gets kids into the game and what keeps them in the game. No matter what other positive reasons to play soccer come along, and there are many – health, socializing, challenges, etc. – if the game is not fun, kids will stop playing.

The other major objective in youth soccer is learning to play the game: patiently and coherently, with technical excellence the major consideration. There will be periods of fast development and periods of slower advancement, but the aim is to keep getting better, year after year.

Coaches should assure the parents that they are going to try to provide as much fun as possible: a relaxed but challenging environment, opportunities to socialize and develop positive personal habits, great activities to play, stimulation and lots of chances to score goals (that's the most fun!) at practice. Movement, running, chasing, shooting, experimenting, making mistakes, supporting one another, laughing about that weird bounce last Saturday, winning a 2 v 2 tournament at practice: that's right!

We should also assure the parents that we're going to play our part in the long, wonderful process by which their child learns to play soccer. Technique is taught at first, learning to control the ball for the youngest players. Then for the older players we blend in tactics and fitness, learning to control the game.

Because it is such a pre-occupation in youth soccer, a few words here about winning. Soccer is a game: the object is to win. Winning is satisfying and pleasing and generally feels better than losing. But many parents have a distorted idea about winning – and that can have a profound effect on their child's enjoyment of and entire experience in soccer. It is vital to remember that when kids are asked to list the reasons they play soccer, poll in and poll out, "Winning" is way down the list for both boys and girls.

Here, let's make some distinctions. We want the kids to get used to competing: that's the nature of sport. We want them to play hard, to do their best, to try always to outplay their immediate opponent and the other team. Soccer is a struggle of competing intentions and forces: we want the kids to train themselves to prevail, and, of course, to accept graciously those times when they can't. That means that we should set up, by the time the kids are U10, maybe, and U12 or U14 for sure, lots of games and activities at practice 'to win': races, 'first to 10' activities, 2 v 2's, 3 v 3's, 4 v 4's. In those situations, winning is important.

Of course, it is also good to win the week's game. But winning the league or a tournament or using a winning season to justify coaching excellence: careful! Those successes are all fine outcomes, if kept in perspective and if thought of in the context of the primary aims: fun and learning.

Winning is often considered inordinately important by the parents; in the worst case, the whole dynamic of their child's involvement is unfortunately reduced to the question of whether or not the team is winning. We coaches should have forthright and open-minded discussions about this issue with our parents to clarify our outlooks and to overcome some questionable attitudes. Here are some opinions that many of us have heard over and over, with a reply:

- *"Our son has a friend whose team was undefeated last season. Their coach must be excellent!"*

  Maybe the coach is excellent, but it is likely that there are other, more important reasons why the team was so successful: the team was simply better (last season, that is) than their opponents, or they 'won ugly', relying on speed or size or strength. In another year or two, when those factors even out, the teams that have been patiently polishing their skills will prevail. It may also be that your town's administrator unwittingly placed the team in the wrong division, so they didn't have the competition they should have. There have even been cases of coaches deliberately placing their team in an easier division: that is wrong on every level.

As for the team being undefeated: no one wants to have a bad record, but it is questionable whether an undefeated season is a justifiable aim in youth soccer. Losing some games is not a bad thing; it almost certainly means that you're playing even competition, it helps the players learn how to handle frustration and accept limitations and defeat graciously, and to be resilient. It also leads to reflection on a coach's part (Why did we lose?).

Now, if your team played strong competition all season and through the skill and savvy and commitment of all the players and some nice coaching won all its games, that's excellent!

◆ *"My daughter's team is winning. They must be making progress."*

Again, maybe: one would hope so. But it may be that they're winning ugly or playing 'down', or because they're bigger and faster this season.

The team may also be winning because the coach is playing the 'better' players more then the other kids. In youth soccer, at all levels and in all situations, every player should be given, to the extent that is possible, as much playing time as every other player. If there are disciplinary matters or chronic absence, that's a different story.

Youth soccer is about individual, personal development – not building up a successful team. That's a complex statement; this is a really subtle issue! A successful team is a valid objective; a good record is satisfying; you definitely want to instill such virtues as team play and support for teammates. But the primary objective is to help every player get better, considering the long term. Kids who don't get sufficient – fair – playing time will not improve as they should, they'll get discouraged, and they'll quit soccer. We simply never know what the future holds, so we must treat the kids the same.

There have been cases where coaches have announced to the parents – and the team – that they're going to build the team around a few dominant players. That line of thinking is surely not valid in youth soccer; it's questionable at any level.

If I was twelve years old and somebody said to me, *"Hey, we're going to get some soccer going here. We're going to organize practices where you can polish up your skills, play lots of little games, and learn how to see and play better. Then on Saturday we'll have a nice game: we'll try our best to stay out of the picture and let you guys have a great game against some other teams"*, I'd say, *"That's the greatest thing I ever heard!"*

2. Youth soccer should not look like adult soccer.

The youngest players weigh a fourth or a fifth of what we do; they're a fraction as tall; their nervous systems and coordination are still developing; their perceptions and social outlooks are limited. Their grasp of space and speed is still forming; they're not that strong; their attention spans and ability to concentrate are underdeveloped.

They haven't played soccer for long, relatively speaking. They're mesmerized by the ball: they often watch only it, and they follow it around as if it were a magnet. They act on this principle, brilliantly expressed in one of the Danish federation's youth manuals: *"Where the ball is, that's where I want to be."* Of course, they're on to something there! They have a notion that there's not much sense in 'staying wide' or 'spreading out' or 'holding their position', because they want the ball! They intuitively know that their teammate may not give them the ball because <u>he</u> intuitively worries about never getting it back! When the ball does come to them, however randomly that may occur, they're thinking, *"OK, stand back, here I come – I'm going to score!"* If they then lose the ball, there's only one thing on their mind: ***Getting it back!***

So in the beginning a 3 v 3 game may in fact be 1 v 3 plus 2 (teammates). The concept of passing is only occasionally, precociously applied. The buzzing cluster of bodies careens around the field. It may be that the 'dribbler' is running towards two opponents while a third opponent watches a jet go by and a teammate waves to her mom. No problem.

As the weeks, months, and years go by, the kids get bigger, stronger, faster, sharper, more skillful, more clever. They begin to feel more confident on the ball. They can look away from it; they realize that if two opponents confront them, then that means Benny is open.

However, for about 10 years, the kids are in a steep learning curve, technically and tactically, and the game will often look a little slow or ragged or aimless. Parents may have a vision of Barcelona or the local college team or the Boston Breakers in their minds and be thinking, *"Hey, Will (an eight year old) is smart and athletic. How come it's so chaotic out there?"*

Patience, patience! They're all smiling; it's coming!

Youth soccer should not look like adult soccer any more than that second grade art class self-portrait should look like a Rembrandt or a fourth grade piano recital should sound like Mozart.

3. Everybody makes mistakes.

It's true: nobody is perfect. Nevertheless, nobody likes to slip up, to forget stuff, to make a bad decision or to use bad judgment. Adults try to avoid mistakes in business and social dealings, of course. Who would want to make a mistake at the shop or office or among friends?

Our adult perceptions and modes of behavior say: *"Mistakes are bad"*. So coaches have to be quite assertive in reminding or convincing the parents to regard the world of sport with a different outlook. In sports, mistakes occur constantly. That is not to say that they are intentional or desirable: it's just the nature of the pressured, competitive, unpredictable world of sports that mistakes will occur. The best hitters in baseball swing and miss a lot, the best shooters in basketball score on only about 50 per cent of their shots, world class soccer players miss the goal entirely as they take penalty shots. That's life. Even the best athletes are inconsistent.

As the years go by, we hope that our players get more confident and skillful and alert, more stable and consistent, that they cut down on their mistakes. In the beginning, though, obvious, blatant mistakes will occur constantly: ball control will be shaky, players will kick the ball randomly, right to the other team; kids will run so hard that they wear themselves out in the first half. (Who's thinking about the second half?)

Coaches have to get used to the endless mistakes that occur in practices or games, and it will make everyone's experience more enjoyable if the parents join in the relaxing. It is striking how worked up many parents get at games, how they're right out there on the field with their child (<u>as</u> their child?), how intensely they get absorbed in the action. A mother bites her lip as her son shoots over the crossbar, a father puffs out his cheeks as his daughter plays a bad pass, several parents sigh, and their shoulders go down as the goalkeeper lets an easy shot go into the net.

Perhaps you could bring up this strangely ironic situation to your parents and ask them to consider it. People go to watch, let's say, arbitrarily, the New England Revolution play the Chicago Fire. With all due respect to the great players on the field, in any given minute it is likely that something like this may occur: a Chicago player passes to a teammate, but the pass is intercepted. The Revolution player who now has the ball tries to dribble past a Fire player, who tackles the ball away from him, but knocks the ball out of bounds. The Revolution throw the ball in, but it's intercepted; the Fire player who took it plays a long ball up to a striker, who fires it over the goal into the stands.

Meanwhile, most people in the stands are watching rather quietly, intuitively knowing that this steady stream of mistakes is the nature of the game. Those same people, at a U10 game the next weekend, are anxious and tense, and may be audibly critical about exactly the same sorts of mistakes that their nine year old sons and daughters make.

We should persist in our attempts to get the parents to relax and accept the inevitable mistakes of the players – not to mention those of the referee and of the coaches. Their kids are going to learn only by making many mistakes. If the kids are tight because coaches or parents yell out during games when they make a mistake or criticize them after games for their mistakes, their development will be profoundly compromised. They won't try new techniques, they'll be more nervous in general, their concentration will be altered, and they won't want to try new positions, especially goalkeeper, for fear of making a mistake.

Some parents may ask you how you can be so complacent about the mistakes their kids are making. *"Won't Daniel get bad habits?"* You can say: *"Sure, he may, but if he keeps playing and practicing, over time he'll work through them. What matters, most of all, is that he keeps playing and playing and playing. All over the world, kids learn to play soccer on their own, make thousands of mistakes, goof up, get some bad habits, make a couple thousand more mistakes. Then they turn pro."*

Kids need encouragement, not criticism. Coaches should ask the parents not to criticize their kids after games, win or lose. It is best just to let the emotions come down and get on with the next activity of the day. Those game reviews in the car on the way home do no good at all. We can set a good example by refraining from having a team meeting after a game, again, win or lose. If the team won, the kids are generally content and are thinking about later in the day. If the team lost, the kids may be momentarily unhappy (often way less unhappy than the coach), they won't be receptive to much of what the coach to say, and the coach may, unintentionally or not, come across as being overly critical. The kids are eager to go after a game; the parents are eager to go. *Let's go!*

If you're concerned that the kids may miss a 'lesson' or forget something: if it's important, they won't forget it, and it can wait a few days. Then when you bring it up at practice, generalize it, as opposed to directing it to or on one player, make your comments and tone constructive, keep it brief.

4. Real soccer

A misconception among many parents is that if the kids are not playing 11 versus 11 games, or at least 8 versus 8 when they're very young, then they are not playing "real soccer". That misunderstanding, unfortunately, is one of the ironies of youth soccer. Many parents have an irrationally negative reaction to six or seven or eight-a-side soccer for the U8's to U12's. Whether or not they've played soccer, they can get quite vociferous about this issue.

- *"When are they ever going to learn positions?"*
- *"How will they understand tactics?"*
- *"They'll never get fit on that little field."*
- *"Won't they be at a competitive disadvantage when they play against kids who have played 11 a side soccer before and are used to it?"*

Not so many years ago, many towns and clubs were rushing their teams into the 11 a side game; the feeling seemed to be 'the sooner the better'. Now, in 2004, more and more programs are playing with smaller numbers longer: 3 v 3 or 4 v 4 for the U6's, 5 v 5 or 6 v 6 for the U8's, 6 v 6 or 7 v 7 for the U10's, and 8 v 8 for the U12's, then 11 v 11 after that. "Eleven after eleven", as they say.

That's a positive step: there are many advantages to playing on smaller fields, as long as possible. The biggest one is that it is possible to play <u>real</u> soccer that involves maximum ball contact for the players, lots of passing, plenty of engagement for everyone, and probably most importantly, a lot of chances to score and, on the other hand, to stop scoring chances by the opponent.

*These smaller games may not qualify in adult eyes as "real"
– but for the kids they're the real deal.*

Here are some thoughts about several of the objections to playing with smaller numbers:

◆ Learning a position will come naturally and intuitively later.
   For a while, the kids are well served if they try to feel the
   different primary functions on the field: scoring if they're up
   front, advancing the ball or helping to defend if they're in
   midfield, winning the ball back by their own goal. For sure,
   the most important priorities from U8 to U12 are to develop
   their techniques and to learn both to attack and to defend.
   If a player is skillful with the ball, can help her or his team to
   keep possession, and shoot well; and on the defensive
   side, win the ball from opponents, she or he will be able to
   play all over the field. If that player is not a good all-round
   ball player, it doesn't matter what position they play: they'll
   struggle.

◆ As for tactics: soccer is a simple game. It is, for sure, free
   and dynamic and unpredictable, but there are recognizable
   patterns and situations, and when you get right down to it,
   they're pretty simple. Learning how to play soccer is much
   like learning anything else: first things first. That means,
   tactically, get involved in lots of 1 v 1 and 2 v 1 and 2 v 2
   duels and learn how to dominate them. Smaller games on
   a smaller field provide many more of these confrontations
   (that is, learning opportunities) than big games do. Kids
   playing in smaller games should be tactically advanced, not
   inhibited. For the sake of perspective: immediately after
   she won the 2004 Wimbledon women's championship,
   Maria Sharapova said, *"I don't know what the tactics were.
   I was just out there. I was just playing."*

◆ And as for fitness: soccer is a start and stop game that
   demands quick, precise movements, agility, and toughness.
   The fact that, in smaller games, the players are always, relatively speaking, near the ball; the constant action; and the
   steady stream of attacking and defending actions and reac-

tions demanded of all the players will produce super-fit soccer players.

Think about this: If I'm the left back on my U12 team, which plays 11-a-side soccer, and our right wing is in possession of the ball, it could easily be 70 yards away from me. I may wait a long time before the ball even comes near me. I'm standing, I'm standing….

Young soccer players are actually well served by the fact that the size of the fields they play on increases incrementally – and dramatically – over the years. If a player starts on a 25 yards by 35 yards field at U6 and graduates to a 60 yards by 100 yards field later, he'll end up playing on a field seven times bigger than the one he played on when he began!

It's a good idea to look around the soccer world to see what's happening. That will often provide us with information that is helpful to us – and to parents. Consider Sweden. In a country which is about as big as California and which has a population about one third that of California, there are 7,900 soccer fields:
 ◆ 3,900 full size grass fields.
 ◆ 2,700 7 v 7 fields (!!)
 ◆ 1,300 gravel fields.

In 2002, the Swedish men's national team got to the quarterfinals of the men's World Cup, in 2004, their women's national team was in the finals of the women's World Cup.
That's compelling.

Kids who play games a little longer on smaller fields have a better, more intense place to develop techniques, they learn to read the game better, and they get soccer fit in a more effective, comprehensive way than kids who have been doing all that long distance running, far from the ball, on the big field. With their skill, savvy, and physical sharpness, they'll adjust quickly to the big field, and they'll soon have a distinct competitive advantage.

5. Youth soccer is not primarily a spectator sport

Youth soccer happens so that kids can have fun, be healthy, learn, try, run, miss, smile, score, recover, scheme, dream, grow strong. It's for playing and participating, not so much for watching. What's most important is that games are for the enjoyment and learning of the players: they should feel, as much as possible, that they are in their own little world, free, dreamy, invented each moment.

That's not to say that a youth soccer game is not enjoyable to watch. A parent can find out so much about their child during a game: how confident they are, how calm and composed – at least as far as soccer goes, how resilient, how gracious when the bounces are going wrong, how dignified when the bounces are going well, how open-minded, how friendly. Soccer games can be another nice window into the life of a child, along with car rides, hikes, suppers or working in the garden.

Coming to observe the joy and earnest efforts and personalities of the kids is wonderful, as long as spectators (parents and coaches) are in the background. The parents should never dominate, audibly or visually; unfortunately, they often do.

As the Swedes say: "Players in the center!"

6. Soccer is just one part of life

Obviously, soccer is great. But it's just one of many worthwhile activities, like learning to play the saxophone, reading, skating, double Dutch, basketball or hip hop dancing. Kids also need time to do nothing, time to dream and gaze and not to be purposeful.

If a kid is crazy about soccer, OK, fine. Let's hope that he loves soccer all his life. Kids usually have a good intuitive sense about how much of anything is enough, and if they don't, then their parents should help them to restore some balance in their lives. Parents should not be the ones who are pushing for more. Our culture is so fast and competitive and acquisitive that many parents think "the more, the better". They don't want their child to miss anything, so they fret about their child making club teams, getting to clinics, going to camp(s), traveling to tournaments. Parental pressure can be counterproductive, too. Most kids who stick with soccer (or other sports) are strong-willed and dynamic. If such a kid gets it into her head that a parent is exerting too much pressure – to win, play extra games, etc. – there could be some push-back, with no positive outcome.

Playing Fall and Spring soccer seasons in town, some at school, a couple of weeks of camp in the summer, throw in a tournament or two: that's plenty. Then there is room for other sports and activities – as well as a very important missing ingredient, pickup soccer – which help to create a well-rounded, resourceful child. Those various pastimes also help to keep kids fresh; they save them from being over-saturated and from getting to the point where one of these activities may start to feel like work.

7. Sporting gestures

Soccer is filled with positive sporting gestures: hand-shakes before the game are now common in many professional leagues, players on one team kick the ball out of bounds to stop the game if an opponent is injured, players trade shirts as a mark of respect at the end of a game.

Relative to the rest of the sporting world, soccer at the highest levels is dignified and civilized; it places high value on fair play and self-control.

Parents and everyone associated with soccer should do all they can to protect the spirit and integrity of the game. It will really help if their sideline demeanor is calm and positive, and there is one particular gesture they can make that will improve the quality of every game.

Parents should be encouraged to applaud all excellent plays, by either team. The intense, partisan atmosphere that shows itself at most pro games, in all sports, has no place in youth sports. Naturally, all parents are most concerned with their own child and his or her performance, and they want to cheer on and encourage their daughter or son. That's human nature, and that's good. But what if they also cheered every time that something exceptional happened, regardless of which team made the play? Our winger puts in a beautiful cross: we cheer. Their goalkeeper makes a sprawling save to stop our striker: we cheer. Our right half puts in a great, long-range shot: we cheer.

It is customary to cheer for our team instead of, or at least more than, for the other team. Wouldn't it be a great example of adult concern, affection, and objectivity if parents at the games cheered for all the kids? The implicit message would be: we appreciate all of you, we're here for all of you. Parents at a dance or music recital applaud everybody; this is not all that different.

If the parents applaud all good plays, a more positive spirit pervades the game. Everyone tends to relax – players, coaches, referees.

8. What kids say

Parents should be aware of what kids do not like about soccer, as well as what they do like. Years ago, Joe Provey, the editor of the excellent magazine <u>Soccer Jr.</u> wrote about their complaints, based on conversations with and letters from many kids and many adults.

Kids said they did not like:
  • Coaches who take things too seriously. Especially bother some were coaches who took winning too seriously.
  • Short-tempered or edgy coaches. Kids also mentioned coaches who did not follow their own advice, like, for example, the ones who preach respect for officials but who are all over referees during games.
  • Being stuck in one position – especially goalkeeper.
  • Coaches who showed favoritism to or were overly tough on their own kids.
  • Coaches who couldn't teach or ran boring practices.
  • Coaches who did not give everyone equal playing time.

- Parents who did not know anything about soccer but who complained or commented as if they did, those who were too vocal or emotional at games, and those who pushed their kids into playing.

Coaches should suggest to parents that they keep talking with their kids about their soccer involvement in a low key, objective, open-minded way.

9. Don't coach during the game

One of the many things that should be addressed in the pre-season parents' meeting is the issue of coaching from the sidelines. The term "coaching" here is considered in the broadest sense: it means any advice at all which is called out to players. Most parents call out only to their own kids, but sometimes there are so many comments coming from the sidelines that, even if the players wanted to listen (and they don't!), they would have a hard time filtering them all out. Is that my dad?

Parents' calling out to the kids during a game distracts them, breaks their concentration, and often puts them in two minds. The advice they are hearing may be completely wrong, it may contradict what the coach has said, and it often adds an unnecessary level of emotion to an atmosphere that is plenty charged already. The players must learn to make their own decisions – that is the essence of soccer – and all these requests or commands inhibit that process. Perhaps most importantly, all the commentary from the sidelines detracts from the players' enjoyment.

It is sometimes necessary to be forceful when talking to parents about this issue: they get emotionally involved in the action, they are tensely anxious about their child's performance, and they may, at least subconsciously, want to control the action. They may also, simply, want to be helpful. They're not sure that their daughter sees the wing who is free, so they yell, "Play it wide!"

Frustrated by the patient buildup of passes in midfield (which is making the coach's day!), they shout to their son, "Send it!", whatever that means. They're getting worried because the team is down a goal late in the game, so every time the ball is within 30 yards of the opponent's goal, they yell *"Shoot!"*.

We should explain to parents that we will give the kids some reminders before the game, make a minimum of comments during the game, and try to address two or three issues, briefly, during halftime. From us coaches, we remind the parents, will come no 'scripting' of the game, no choreography, no constant calibrating and tuning, and no post-game analysis to the team. The parents should see us talking to the subs, taking a few notes, calling out a very occasional question or comment, and calmly encouraging everybody. If they want to cheer all the kids or make a positive remark after a play is made, that's fine.

This may be a tough issue for you: it may be one of those times when it is not so easy to take your own advice! But there are many advantages to being as quiet as possible on the side-lines during games. Your players, who understand your approach, will, of course, be grateful. Now they can do their own thinking, play their game without all those distracting comments and enjoy their freedom!

The parents may not understand your design, and they may come at you with questions: Why are you so passive? Don't the kids need (deserve, rely on) your instructions? Aren't they at a disadvantage if you don't help them during the game? Look at that coach over there (the one leaning forward, pointing, offering a stream of advice to his players). Don't those kids have an edge on us today?

And maybe in the back of your mind is the static that says: maybe the kids would be better served if I talked or instructed – or yelled – more. There may even be situations where you think: How can I not call out to them about this? A winger is wide open as a halfback receives the ball, or neither wingback remembers to set up to protect the posts on a corner kick, or your back line is playing too far back and not moving up well, etc. You may feel self-conscious, thinking that maybe the parents will think you actually don't know what to say.

Don't worry. The advantages to saying as little as possible will begin to show themselves immediately, and they will lead to far better players in the long run.

Stress to the parents that kids left to play on their own, except for a very few brief, well-chosen comments, will most likely:
  • Learn to think for themselves, concentrate better, and become more self-reliant.
  • Talk with and help their teammates and understand how vital communication on the field, within the team, really is.
  • Value and pay more attention to your comments at half-time and at the next practice.
  • Some – perhaps many – will become leaders.
  • Realize that success in the game relies on their dynamic, free, and constant thinking and acting, their 'reading' the endless flow of possibilities, and then seizing the moment.
  • Have a whole lot more FUN!

Finally, we should assure the parents that we want the game to be loud – but that the noise should come from the players. Too many youth soccer games are backwards: the players are listening to the sidelines (or trying not to listen), and the sidelines are a noisy source of comments, commands, and edgy opinions. The players should be communicating with one another and picking up an occasional suggestion or question from the coach; the parents should be cheering or listening.

10. Kids should play all the positions

In modern soccer, everybody should know how to attack and defend, pass, tackle, and shoot. So much the better if they know something about goalkeeping. All the players should be capable and clever and dangerous with the ball and strong and helpful without it. It's simple: if you're not so good with the ball, then you're always trying to get rid of it, or you'll lose it anyway. If you're not good at forcing the other team into errors or at winning the ball, then your teammates have to do all the defending.

There is another important reason why kids should play all over the field, in 'all the positions': to learn the different types of thinking involved. In soccer, opponents do not so much over-power the players on the other team as out-think and 'out-skill' them. Out-thinking an opponent has a lot to do with getting inside their head, seeing what they see, imagining the possibili-ties they imagine. If I play on the wing sometimes, it is easier for me to imagine what my opponent is plotting when I later end up playing right back. If I take my turn in the goal as a goalkeeper from time to time, I will know how hard it is, the next time I end up playing as a striker, to stop a ball driven low and hard just inside the far post.

The Brazilian national teams – both women and men – are known for their beautiful technique and flair and fantasy. They also play great defense, and one of the reasons for that is that they know all about what their opponents are thinking when they have the ball.

Some parents have a one dimensional outlook: they hope their child is the big scorer, or they wonder which position best suits their tall, fast-growing 10 year old, or somebody told them that their 11 year old daughter had the makings of a great goal-keeper. They may be of the opinion that kids get good at a posi-tion only by starting there early and playing there as much as possible.

We should assert to the parents that it is best for the play-ers to play all over the field, get a feel for the different 'climates', use their techniques to solve the problems that occur in different areas of the field, and explore the possibilities. Then, at U14 or U16, they'll probably gravitate to one position or 'line' or other; in any case, the more flexible and resourceful they have become, the better.

11. Get involved

As the years go by, more and more of the parents of our players have played soccer and know about the game. Some parents, on the other hand, never played and don't know the game.

Others never played but have been watching their two sons play for five years now, and they're getting a good sense of the game.

Whatever their background and experience, all the parents can derive or continue to derive great enjoyment and satisfaction from soccer and can contribute to its growth and stability.

Coaches should educate them about all the possibilities for enjoyment of and engagement in youth soccer:

- Coaching, or maybe at first, assistant coaching.
- Administrating: serving on a town's or club's board of directors, acting as their organization's coach education director, or becoming an age-level coordinator. Organizations need people with managerial smarts, those with financial brains, visionaries, fund raisers, those with big garages and basements. If a lot of good-hearted people did not step up to line fields, store goals, hand out equipment, and register players, youth soccer would be gone.
- Refereeing. Soccer needs every good referee it can get.
- Those parents who do not have a soccer background can consider reading about the game or taking a coaching course or a referee's course to educate themselves.
- Watching soccer on television is a good way to learn about soccer, too. There is more and more access to soccer on television now – to all its excitement and beauty. And if we want the telecasts to continue, we in the soccer community must express our appreciation – by tuning in.
- Support local soccer teams: high school and college, semi-pro and full professional. We must all contribute to make sure that the soccer culture flourishes.

Chapter Four

11 Ways to Improve Your Town or Club Organization

In youth soccer, many town programs or club organizations are run by committed, dynamic, charismatic individuals or small groups of people. As long as those people are present, everything goes along fine, but whenever they decide to retire, or they burn out because they are overburdened, the town or club is in trouble. A town or club should be sure that its structure is solid and is not overly dependent on any person or small group of people.

Naturally, there is tremendous diversity among youth soccer entities. There are large, well organized, ambitious ones; newly begun, small ones; cordial ones; contentious ones. Some are directed by idealistic philosophers who want to design a sound social and athletic environment, others by short-sighted and inexperienced coaches who want to win trophies. Let's say that your club is established responsibly, with all the proper registration work in place, tax exempt status, a good-hearted board of directors or a good-hearted group of leaders. Then what? What are your objectives, hopes, methods of advancing?

Here are 11 guidelines for you to consider as you seek to improve your town or club program. (Here "town" means the combination of recreational and travel teams sponsored by a town's affiliated soccer organization; "club" means the private, select, competitive teams that draw players from many towns.) These are the kinds of issues that a good board will be thinking about all the time. You could help your board a great deal by aiding them in their deliberations or by volunteering to help with some of these initiatives.

1. Train coaches

Educated, progressive, cultivated coaches are the most important resource for a soccer program. The first priority for any town or club should be to train its coaches systematically and as thoroughly as possible.

An astute organization arranges coaching courses annually for its coaches – either through its state's youth soccer organization, or a local professional organization, or through a member of the organization who is competent to teach others. New coaches should be offered coaching support before they have to meet the kids on the field, for their enjoyment and peace of mind and confidence, as well as to be sure that they are at least minimally qualified to lead a team. It doesn't take much to prepare someone to be a competent activity leader or a beginning coach. A half day spent talking about and practicing the organization of time and space; and learning about sound objectives for young players, the components of soccer, and some great games is a fine start. It's amazing how many coaches come to a state G Course or Youth Module and say, *"I've been coaching for four (or nine) years, but I've never taken a course like this."* And almost always they leave shaking their head, commenting, *"If I'd only had this from the start!"*

Your town or club can make its own plan or, even better, get together with another town or club and make a schedule for hosting various offerings. For example, you and a neighboring town might decide:
- This August, you'll host a G Course or a Youth Module.
- In September, one of your coaches, a vastly experienced guy with talent for teaching, will present two 90 minute workshops on practice activities: nice shooting exercises, conditioned small sided games, various ways to play keep away, etc. In October, one of their coaches, a former college goalkeeper with lots of enthusiasm for teaching, will present two 90 minute sessions on how to help U12 and U14 kids be better keepers.
- Next March, they'll host a pre-Spring season F Course or a second Youth Module.

- During next Spring's season, you'll each host a local college coach one night for 90 minutes: one night she'll talk about games to help U10 players improve their techniques; the second night she'll talk about systems of play and tactics for the 11-a-side game.
- Next August, you'll host an E Course, and through the Fall season there will be a series of mini-clinics in both towns, presented by eager and resourceful coaches whom you and your neighbor have identified.
- Nice year!
- And so forth.

While it is great to have good fields, an array of goals and gear and snappy uniforms, well trained coaches are far more important than any or all of these elements.

The organization should especially support new coaches. Volunteer coaches are involved in youth soccer purely out of the goodness of their hearts. And as enjoyable and fulfilling as it is to coach kids' soccer, it can strain an already busy schedule; it can even become disruptive to family life. Preparing practice sessions, leading practices, and then guiding the team on game day can involve a considerable amount of time. For most people, too, coaching is a new and quite challenging endeavor, satisfying and stimulating for sure, but far different from most of their other activities.

A town or club organization can help its new coaches to enjoy their experience and to be much more effective leaders if it takes a few simple steps:
- Provide all new coaches with a mentor or advisor. The organization can pair people up, or ask one experienced and good-hearted coach to be available for phone calls or emails from several new ones. This would be an informal arrangement, not at all intended to take the place of opportunities for coach education which the town is also, one would hope, arranging. The mentor is just a supportive presence, a resource, a friendly and helpful guide. New coaches could ask about issues of diplomacy, a new shooting activity, some approaches for a team that has lost four

games in a row, how to convince a worried parent that heading is safe.

- Encourage your experienced coaches to keep a record of their practice sessions – and then pass them on. Nothing fancy or formal here: that 'record' could simply be 20 or 30 three by five cards on which the coach made his practice plans, tucked into a folder. Or it could be 18 or 20 sheets of paper, the past year's practices, in a manila envelope. The experienced coach could pass on this resource (a piece of gold!) to a new coach by way of showing her what is a reasonable amount to plan each session, how simple planning practice is, how a year's practices flow. If I was a new U10 coach and someone handed me 24 detailed practice plans that they had made for their U10 team the previous year, I'd be very happy.
- Say to the new coaches, *"In a year or two, you can return the favor!"*
- If your organization has a Coach Education Director and a Technical Director (it should have both!), ask them to make themselves available from time to time at evening practices, just to drop in toward the end of practices so that new or not so new coaches could ask them questions or express opinions.

A town or club must be realistic about the amount of money that its coaches are willing to devote to advancing as a coach. The town or club should, though, do all it can to organize consistent educational opportunities, to offer access to books and tapes, and to inspire coaches to keep moving forward.

2. State your philosophy and your principles and ask coaches and parents to follow them

A clear, coherent philosophy and consistent principles are vital for all towns and clubs. A strong philosophical and cultural basis is essential if you want to teach soccer well. In some towns, there are strong, direct expressions of youth soccer intentions and objectives; these serve to guide and unify everyone. As the players – and the parents – move from one team to the next, the feeling is essentially the same, the approaches and priorities similar. The players benefit from a well-considered, logical, consistent soccer education. In other towns, there are no consistent guidelines and policies, and the experience for the young players is not what it should be.

Since sport always springs out of culture, it is important to consider your community's or club's cultural environment as you devise these guidelines. Most of the philosophical grounding and the methods of a youth soccer organization are obvious, intuitive, and generic; but they are also influenced by cultural differences. Is your soccer organization established and solid, young and evolving, or brand new? Is the feeling among the parents assertive and competitive, laid back or a challenging mix of the two? Are people within your organization willing and dynamic volunteers or rather passive, even skeptical? Is soccer the big sport in your community or one of many competing sports? Does your organization have solid funding? These are typical 'cultural' questions, and, given the great variety of social and economic settings in America, there may be others.

Here are some broad suggestions to consider as a basis for an expression of philosophy; these should be refined with attention to your particular culture:

- Our organization exists to enable kids to learn to play soccer and to enjoy the world's most popular sport. We want to promote a love of the sport, good health, and a friendly environment.
- We consider our coaches primarily as teachers: of techniques and tactics, of sound sporting attitudes, of respect for soccer and the spirit of athletics. We expect them to be impeccable models of sportsmanship, always placing the welfare of the players and concern for their social and athletic educations foremost. Any behavior that would be inappropriate in a school classroom is inappropriate at our soccer practices and games. Raised voices, harsh or critical language, comments that blame kids for mistakes (Can you imagine any of these in a classroom?): all are unacceptable.
- We would like players to be respectful, upright, and open-minded at practices and games.

- We expect parents to be positive, supportive, and friendly among the players and other parents and toward the coach.
- Our primary focus is educational, our secondary one competitive. (For some clubs, at least with regard to some age groups, that statement may be backwards.) We want the players to have enjoyable, fair, appropriate competition; but our first consideration is that they all learn to play soccer to the best of their abilities. That means, among other things, that we're going to stress practice and training and keep the practice to games ratio correct: more practices than games, that is. It also means that we're going to attend only a few tournaments. Instead of spending our town's or club's savings on tournament fees and asking parents to spend considerable money attending tournaments, we're going to invest that money on coach education, small goals, and books and tapes for our club library.

These broad statements can be supported by as much detail as your town or club wishes. Having these guidelines in place will be good for everyone. Coaches will have a clear idea of their role and function and will feel supported. Parents, especially those who are new to soccer, will know what the aims and priorities of the organization are.

In practical terms, too, having a clear philosophy in place will be very helpful. A classic problem within a town or club is a coach who is out of tune or a parent who consistently behaves in an inappropriate way. The coach may be one of those "knows his soccer but he's tough on the kids, and you should hear him with the refs" types. If the Board or the leaders of the town or club need to approach this coach to ask him to modify his behavior, or, in a more extreme case, to remove him, they can do so more confidently and fairly with their organization's explicit philosophy in hand. And if a coach is compelled to address an over-the-top parent about sideline behavior, she or he can do so more forcefully by appealing to the guidelines to which everyone has been asked to conform.

A clear statement of ideals and purposes is needed more than ever in our competitive culture. There have been examples of home teams letting the grass grow extra long or watering down the fields to frustrate opponents. It is dismaying that those kinds of actions are even considered.

Soccer is an art form, and as such it is a subject of opinion. For everyone's maximum enjoyment and peace of mind, make your opinions clear.

3. Compose a simple, general frame for age-level objectives for your players.

Imagine a school where the third grade teacher was presenting harder math than the fourth grade teacher, where the sixth grade and seventh grade teachers never talked to one another about their English curriculums, where a fourth grade science teacher continually used difficult, abstract language.

Everyone – players and coaches – will be better served if your organization has a coherent expression of age-appropriate aims. In almost all circumstances, a basic, generalized design is sufficient, as opposed to a detailed "curriculum". This framework is helpful for leaders and coaches, especially those rather inexperienced ones who naturally wonder, "What should I do?" with their teams, at every level. A time line such as this will give them some support in understanding what would happen organically – and actually does happen in many parts of the world – if kids were just left to play soccer and develop without the intervention of a coach.

There are several clarifications and qualifications to be made about this frame of objectives:
  ◆ These suggestions, which are extremely difficult to express in words and which are nearly impossible to quantify, are all general. Because each child is unique, no two children will ever master the elements of the game in the same way. There are big 10 year olds, small ones, dreamy nine year olds, clever ones, precocious eight year olds, rebellious 12 year olds, superb athletes, kids who just want to hang out and kick around with their friends. And kids don't always develop in a straight line: there will be times when they may be adjusting to their new bodies, when they are socially

awkward, when they may be a little defiant. And, of course, every one of them will be inconsistent, will make countless mistakes and will have bad days.

- None of these ideas should be considered to suggest an end result or a finished product. Players develop over many years. The process is open ended and sometimes erratic and never really "done". There are many invisible, rather mysterious, elusive qualities, such as persistence, concentration, and imagination, that are vital for success, different from child to child, and impossible to measure.

- Typically, your team will be composed of three groups of kids: those who are 'ahead' of these aims, the few very coordinated and motivated ones who are your (momentarily!) best players; some who will struggle to play as well as the majority of kids on the team; and the largest, middle group of 'average' players. You may think: I can't wait until I get a team where all the players have the same skill level. Unfortunately, it's doubtful that any team is actually like that. It is more likely that each team is composed, more or less, of those same three groups. April Heinrichs and Bruce Arena would probably agree: on their national teams they have a few stars; a few who may play a couple of games with the team and show themselves incapable of performing at that level; and the majority of the team, 'average' players at that level.

- As satisfying as it is to develop and advance, most players come to practice just to play, to have fun, to be with friends, to be stimulated and challenged today. Few players have the kind of informed, long-term vision that leaders and coaches should cultivate.

- This kind of frame can also serve the purpose of suggesting to leaders and coaches what not to do at various age levels. Many coaches are overly ambitious and get into tactics and set plays before the kids can control the ball and read fundamental situations. Take your cue from how your practice games and scrimmages look. What kinds of movements and skills and decisions are happening? Heading with seven year olds? No. Suggesting to your nine year olds that they kick the ball over to the other side of the field (40 yards) to attack down the other wing? Of course not, but it happens.

Here is a simple frame of technical and tactical aims for kids from U6 to U14. There is nothing here about fitness: the implicit understanding is that practicing vigorously and playing games will help kids to get more agile, balanced, and soccer-fit. Your organization may want to make this more specific or detailed, but remember: simplicity is always best.

Remember, also: playing is most important. If you are ever in doubt about what to do with your players, separate the kids into small teams and play a game. You can't go wrong if the kids are playing a soccer game.

U6: Me and my rolly ball, in the grass.

Here we go! Lots of touching the ball, guiding it, stopping it, turning it, beginning to become, as the Swedes say, "friends with the ball", beginning to learn how it rolls. Kicking (not "passing" – there's no such thing yet) the ball reasonably straight over eight to 10 yards. Getting good on the feet, with the feet.

At practice: dribbling activities, tag, relays, 1 v 1, 2 v 2, 3 v 3, maybe 4 v 4.

Please, NO: tactics beyond the simplest 'weekly game organization' (which usually unravels as soon as the game begins), stretching, calinsthetics, goalkeeper stuff (no need for a keeper in their game), running, big discussion of the rules (they have an innate sense of fairness; if they push one another, ask them not to do that; no need for a referee in their weekly game), heading.

U8: Soccer is fun!

As many ball touches as possible. Guiding and moving and stopping the ball with the insides, outsides, and bottoms of the feet. Controlling rolling balls with the insides and outsides of both feet; beginning to understand how important "first touch" is in maintaining possession of the ball. Reasonably accurate 'passes' (that word begins to have some meaning now) of eight to 12 yards.

Introduction of some fundamental tactical ideas: Try to protect the ball. Let's spread out when we have the ball. Let's come a little closer to one another if we lose it, and let's protect the area in front of our goal. Let's shoot a lot! If we lose the ball, let's chase after it right away!

At practice: dribbling, tag, relays, target games, 1 v 1, 2 v 2, 3 v 3, 4 v 4. Just enough about the rules to keep everything right and moving fast.

Please, NO: big tactics, stretching, running without the ball, calinsthetics, goalkeeper 'training' beyond how to move your hands to stop a rolling ball, time on set plays, heading.

U10: This is cool!

Guiding and turning the ball with the insides, outsides, and bottoms of the feet. Several ways to turn: stop the ball with the bottom of your foot and spin, cut it back with the inside of the foot or the laces, cut it back with the outside of the foot, pull it back with the sole of the foot. Changes of speed and direction with the ball, feints, and moves to beat opponents (simple ones, like pulling the ball across your body with the inside of the foot or flicking it the other way with the outside of the foot and then running past the defender). Accurate ground passes over 15 to 20 yards with the insides of the feet and the laces. Receiving balls while moving and setting up the next action (dribble, shoot, or pass) with a good first touch. Understanding that receiving the ball is just a means to an end. Protecting the ball ("shielding") effectively. Shooting with the insides of the feet and the laces and keeping the ball inside the frame of the goal. Technical points about the hands and about the footwork involved in goal-keeping; how to roll, throw, and punt the ball. Techniques of tackling.

At practice: dribbling, passing, and receiving, keepaway, playing in pressured spaces. Learning the fundamentals of heading – but practicing that skill very little. Shooting every session, and everybody playing in the goal at every session. 1 v 1, 2 v 1, 2 v 2, 3 v 3, 4 v 4.

Tactics: now there are lots of ideas to bring in. Players should be encouraged to look around all the time, both on attack and defense. They should learn to recognize, for example, when they are under pressure and when they are not under pressure when they receive a pass or when the ball comes to them. Also: the importance of moving to the ball, of playing it away from pressure, of helping the player with the ball ("Go to help!", "Ask for the ball!", etc.), of getting away from defenders. Consistently getting in between opponents, whether they are in possession of the ball or not, and your own goal when you've lost the ball. Simple 2 v 1 combinations: the wall pass, the 1 – 2. Knowing the difference between passes to feet and passes to space. Shooting at every opportunity. Beginning to understand the notion (from the Dutch) of the four "main moments" of soccer: possession by the opponent, transition as we win the ball, our possession, and transition as our opponent wins the ball back from us. Making the field big when we have the ball, compressing it when we lose it. Hunting and pressing the ball on defense and covering (helping out) the pressing defender. Rudimentary 'position play' and functions in the team. The minimum about set plays.

Please, NO: running without the ball – except in tag and relays, long lectures, specializing by positions, emphasis on winning.

U12: "Man on, Dennis! Here's help!"

Turning cleverly and quickly. Learning and practicing moves to beat defenders: changing speed and direction and being deceptive. Shielding well and learning to use the shoulders to win and keep the ball. Accurate ground passes and air balls over 20 yards; learning to chip the ball and pass with the outside of the foot. Playing a good first touch consistently after receiving a ground ball. Practicing receiving and shooting air balls; shooting balls off the dribble inside the near and far posts. Tackling well. Everyone continuing to learn about goalkeeping: hand positions and body shape for all shots and crosses; footwork across the goal and out into the field; distribution by rolling, throwing, and punting. A little heading practice.

At practice: some isolated technical practice, at speed and sometimes under pressure. Lots of duels and compressed small games: 1 v 1, 2 v 1, 2 v 2, 3 v 3, 4 v 2, 5 v 2, 4 v 4.

Tactics: emphasis on reading the game and decision making; continuing to stress the four 'moments' of the game. Learning key visual cues: trying to move the ball ahead ("penetrate") when there is no pressure, protecting the ball if there is. Good body position, facing the field and 'open' when asking for the ball. Defending with good, 'half-turned' footwork. Understanding of the climates in different areas of the field and the way to assess safety and risk in each of them. Grasping the difference between losing the ball and giving it away. Moving around the field as a team: opening up or closing off space. Continuing to learn, patiently, the tactics of 1 v 1, 2 v 1, and 2 v 2 with and without the ball. Trying to communicate well.

Please, NO: running for running's sake, long lectures, specializing by positions (especially goalkeeper), emphasis on winning.

U14: "Let's have a nice game!"

Stable, fluid receiving of ground and air balls. Sharp, quick turns; a few dependable moves to beat defenders; strong and stable shielding techniques. Solid tackling, heading after jumping, ability to head the ball up or down. Passing on the ground is accurate over 20 yards; driven air balls are accurate over 25 yards. Shooting is consistently on target, aimed just inside the posts, off the dribble, from ground passes, and from flighted crosses. Goalkeepers now are good at stopping shots inside the frame of the goal, stopping breakaways, catching crosses, and distributing the ball.

At practice: some isolated technical stuff, but mostly fast-paced competitive duels and small games. Emphasis is on using techniques to solve tactical problems, to outplay opponents. Now players start to specialize a little by position, but everyone tries to play more than one – especially the goalkeepers.

Tactics: bringing a sharp, alert attitude to practice and games, trying to think ahead, being aware of game situations and the variables, being deceptive, making good choices about when to dribble, shoot, and pass. Understanding the roles of the players in the three 'blocks' of the field: forwards, midfielders, and backs – including the keeper. Ways to make and use space for yourself and with a teammate, knowing several ways to combine with a teammate to beat an opponent: wall pass, 1 – 2, overlap, take-over; beginning to look for the 'third man running' – or being that third player running – a little in the distance. Confidence and secure tactical sense about shooting. Playing smart individual defense: understanding priorities (intercept, get to the ball as the opponent does and put her under pressure, lure her into exposing the ball). Understanding pressure, cover (the 'second', supporting defender), and balance (the 'third' defender who keeps her eye on opponents and space away from the ball).   Exposure to more than one system: being able to play 4 – 3 – 3 and 3 – 4 – 3, for example. Sharpening up verbal and non-verbal communication. Playing hard and by the rules, understanding offside.

Please, NO: running for its own sake, strength or endurance work, long lectures, emphasis on standings or tournament outcomes.

If your town or club can get a frame like this out into the hands of all the coaches and ask them all to follow it, it will be of great benefit to the coaches and, most importantly, to the players. A frame like this will make it more likely that the youngest (U6 and U8) players will develop their ball skills, that the 'middle' (U10 and U12) players will refine their ball skills and get smart, and that the older (U14) players will then be able to use their solid skills to outplay their opponents on the big field.

This kind of frame will also act as a point of reference if some of the town's or club's coaches are doing inappropriate activities, which, unfortunately, may be the case. U8's practicing heading, U12's passing the ball back and forth while standing still, U10's listening to a long tactical lecture, U14's standing in a line, then dribbling through cones from 40 yards out to take a shot from the edge of the penalty area, one at a time: Please, NO!

If your town or club can get everybody on the same wave length, more or less, the kids will flourish. Here's an image:

It's Tuesday evening on one of your town's practice fields. Over there, a U6 team is buzzing around, all the kids dribbling their ball in a grid as the leader is calling out encouragement; now he's getting them into squares for the Traveling game. Past them, a U14 team is playing two games of 5 v 2. Their coach is standing between the two play areas; occasionally she stops both games and asks a question or offers a suggestion. Two extra players are juggling a ball back and forth, off to the side. On this side, a U8 team has a 2 v 2 'tournament' going; the coach is smiling and clapping her hands and cruising around the perimeter of the fields to praise good plays. Next to them a U10 team is playing two games of 3 v 3. Their coach just pulled everyone together and asked them to use what they were practicing earlier (shielding, in two activities) to protect the ball as they now played.

The predominant sound is the animated communication among the players. A couple of the U10's are cartwheeling now; one of the U6's just sat on his ball; parents are talking in small groups; a couple of the parents are juggling a ball over there.

Youth soccer paradise!

4. Get your town or club involved with TOPSoccer and Special Olympics Soccer

These two organizations do fantastic work and deserve all the help we can give them.

TOPSoccer is The Outreach Program for Soccer: it is administered by US Youth Soccer. A TOPS player is *"any youth player between the ages of four and 19 who has a disability that limits his or her ability to perform at the level of play in which he or she has chosen to participate."* These players may, for example, be visually impaired or hearing impaired, may use a wheelchair, or have mental retardation. Please contact US Youth Soccer (1717 Firman Drive, Suite 900, Richardson, Texas 75081 – 800 4SOCCER – www.youthsoccer.org) for information.

Special Olympics serves people with mental retardation; it is the largest amateur sports organization in the world. Special Olympics stresses participation and personal achievement: its motto is, "Let me win; but if I cannot win, let me be brave in the attempt." Please contact them at Special Olympics, Inc. North America (1325 G Street NW, Suite 770, Washington, D.C. 20005 – 202 628-3630) or through your state's Special Olympics' office.

Soccer for everyone, everywhere!

5. Help your coaches to learn about the prevention and care of injuries and about nutrition.

Youth coaches do not need to become experts in physiology, but they should learn something about sports injuries so that they can, if possible, prevent them, and, if they happen, know how to deal with them. They should also learn about nutrition, so that they can advise their players.

There are many ways your town or club can help:
* See if your local hospital or a local pediatrician will present a session on sports injuries.
* Request that your coaches take a First Aid and a CPR Course.
* Keep your eyes out for articles in newspapers or magazines or on the web about sports fitness and nutrition.
* Model good habits yourself: let the players see you warming up a little, eating right on game or tournament days, drinking plenty of water or sports drink.
* Be very alert on hot, muggy days; if there is even the most remote hint of lightning in the distance; if the field surface is questionable.

6. Invest in gear and hardware

Towns and clubs that invest wisely in coaching aids present their coaches and players with several advantages. Coaches who are dressed well are generally better motivated, and the fact that they have on town or club 'colors' contributes to a feeling of unity and purposefulness. How a coach looks is not superficial; it is no less important than how the players look. Part of being an effective coach is being well equipped; with the proper equipment, a coach can do more. It's that simple. Good, sturdy equipment – and plenty of it – lends an aura of authority and genuine soccer-ness to the environment. This is even more important if the practice and game locations are also baseball or football fields and if they're surrounded by basketball or tennis courts. The more soccer feeling we can get into the air, the better. We should be doing everything we can to improve, materially, what Bruce Arena calls "the day to day soccer environment".

The more gear and hardware, the better for the kids, too. They'll have crisper practice forms and, very important, more goals to shoot at. Real goals, with nets, are vital. Think of how much more satisfying it is to swish a shot through a basketball net than it is to put the ball through the hoop, silently and without that exclamatory movement of the twine. Hitting the net in soccer is a great sensation - and the more the kids can do it and get used to it, the better. Real goalposts and real crossbars – no matter what size the goal is – and real nets are all part of the mystique.

None of this is to suggest that soccer organizations should go looking for fanciful reasons to spend money or that they make impulsive purchases – or that they give gear and equipment to coaches who either don't know what to do with it or aren't inclined to use it.

On the other hand, if you put a sufficient amount of good gear into the hands of a trained coach: now we're talking.

In Chapter Five is the suggestion that coaches "invest in a little gear". That's a good idea if the town or club does not have the means to provide it, but if they do have the means, they should outfit the coach. A town or club would be wise to provide each coach with:

- A polo shirt or two and a hat – all with the town's or club's logo.
- A small training bag or drawstring sack to hold everything.
- A first aid kit.
- 16 or 20 small disc cones.
- Eight large disc cones.
- A ball pump.
- Two or three mini-balls.
- Enough pinnies of two colors so that you can split your squad into thirds: blue team, yellow team, and no pinnies' team.

A further suggestion: The town's or club's gear manager should give everything out just before the Fall season and record who gets what. Then, if your town can afford it, don't ask for anything back – right away. That means that your town or club is making an investment in that coach, and, at the same time, making their logistical life easier. Say to the coaches: All of this gear is yours as long as you coach with us. We're not going to collect anything in the Spring – unless you decide to stop coaching. Then we'll be happy to get back the coaching equipment. Otherwise, every year we will give you another shirt or two and another hat. The training bag and first aid kit are yours to keep. We'll replace items in the first aid kit (band aids, tape, etc.) as you need them. Please be careful of your pump and discs and cones: those are your lifetime supply. We'll replace pinnies every Fall, as you need them.

Then, depending on the organization's resources and ambition and situation, turn your attention to small goals. There are, unfortunately, sometimes issues of security as far as goals go, but if you can figure out a way to keep them safe, the more small goals (4' x 6', 6' x 12', etc.) you have on hand, the better. It's amazing how much small goals can enhance a training session, how much more they enable you to do.

An excellent source of gear and hardware is the company Kwik Goal: 140 Pacific Drive, Quakertown, PA. 18951; 800 531-4252; www.kwikgoal.com.

7. Devise a year-round schedule for players

Life in America is fast, complex, and filled with pressure. There never seems to be enough time, everyone has multiple interests and responsibilities, and families are on the go seven days a week. The calendars of young athletes are particularly complicated and difficult.

It will be helpful for everyone – players, parents, and coaches – if the organization constructs a year-round schedule of soccer activities, at least as a suggested guideline. These schedules will differ, of course, for kids of various ages and motivations, and according to whether your organization is a town's soccer program or a big, ambitious club. These guidelines, for example, are not intended for U6 or U8 players – only for those U10 to U14. The 'soccer year' for a U6 or U8 player should be a simple proposition: Fall season, Spring season, and a week or two at a half day summer soccer camp. And, of course, the park is always waiting for you. This issue is further complicated by the fact that, because of widely differing climates, the 'seasons' in various parts of the country can vary widely. It is, however, possible to make some generalities about a year in soccer – then you can tailor these ideas to fit your own circumstance.

Here is a hypothetical year for a town or club in the Northeast that plays Fall and Spring seasons:
- January: Nothing.
- February and March: Some opportunities to play and some clinics during the February school vacation week, and some indoor soccer – but not necessarily in a competitive "with boards" setting. Two suggestions:

1. If the kids play inside, have them play futsal, inside lines – nothing off the boards.
2. And instead of just signing up for several weeks of a competitive mini-season, you and some parents could investigate the possibility of renting some hours at an indoor facility (check out insurance issues), roll a ball out, and let the kids play pickup for an hour.

- April and May and June: Spring season play, with a mandatory practice or two a week, and perhaps a voluntary one, too. In June, host a small, end-of-season Memorial Day 'soccer festival' for your U10 teams and some from neighboring towns. Each team has three abbreviated (30 minute) games on one day. Scores are kept, but not standings.
- July and August: Pickup games and summer camp possibilities.
- September and October and November: Fall season, with a mandatory practice or two each week. Encourage your U12 and U14 teams to go to a Columbus Day tournament.
- December: Nothing.

Of course, all the soccer the kids want to play on their own – little games, kicking a ball against a wall, juggling – can be happily added to the calendar.

8. Contribute a soccer section to your town library

Libraries and bookstores are more resourceful and better stocked all the time when it comes to soccer books. Still, most librarians are not experts at soccer, and most libraries have a limited amount of money to spend on their whole sports section, much less just soccer books and tapes. You can contribute dramatically to your town's soccer culture and to the education of your town's coaches if you donate soccer books and tapes to your local library.

Here's a nice plan: Go to see one of the librarians at your library. Say: Our organization will be happy to donate soccer books and tapes to the library if you'll catalog them and circulate them. Then convene a group of your coaches or leaders who are familiar with soccer books and tapes that are relevant for your organization's needs and plan an order. (You may want to refer to the appendix of this book for some suggestions.)

Your library may even agree to make a special display of the new materials when they arrive – or just before the next season. To help your coaches, you can hand out a one page listing of all the books and tapes, perhaps with a one-liner about each, to indicate the target audience, style, 'difficulty', etc.

Everybody should be reading a soccer book, all the time!

9. Be sure to have a goalkeeping specialist

All the players should be introduced to the techniques and tactics of goalkeeping. When they are seven or eight, they can jump into the goal during practice activities or games and 'feel' the position, check it out, get a sense of its uniqueness. No need for them to encounter much coaching then – maybe just a few rudiments. Let them simply experience being in front of the goal and understand how tough it is to defend that vital area behind them – and in front of them – and how challenging it is to stop that ball that comes flying at them.

Then when the players are nine or ten, they can begin to practice as goalkeepers at every practice session (yes, every one!) in isolated exercises, in small sided games, and in the day's scrimmage. They should continue to do that – to play a little as a goalkeeper each practice session – through their U14 years. When the players are at the U12 and U14 levels, we should be sure that they are learning about goalkeeping and that as many of them as possible are playing in the goal during the weekly game. None of them should ever play more than half the game. If you have four kids who are interested in playing in the goal during games, and that's a good number to aim for, then each of them should play one half of every other game in the goal. This way, they have a fine experience in the goal, and they also get plenty of playing time out on the field.

Even for coaches who have played soccer before –
unless they were goalkeepers – coaching the techniques and tactics of goalkeeping is a challenge. And, of course, leaders or
coaches new to the game know nothing about it. So a goalkeeping expert is vital for your town or club. She or he can:

- Present occasional mini-clinics to explain and demonstrate
  techniques and tactical concepts.
- Suggest and model isolated exercises that coaches can
  work into the warm-ups or bodies of their practices.
- Drop into practices from time to time to work with the keepers (or all the players) for a few minutes.
- Schedule special training sessions with the U12 and U14
  players who are particularly interested in goalkeeping.
- Help coaches to choose books and tapes about goalkeeping and help select books and tapes that will be in your
  town's library.

*America is known for producing great goalkeepers. Let's
make thousands more!*

10. Organize a shoe and gear recycling system

One of the wonderful aspects of soccer is that it is relatively inexpensive to play: that helps to keep it accessible to
almost everyone. Reduced to its simplest requirement, if a group
of people had just one ball, they could have a game.

For most kids involved in soccer, though, there are more
material needs than just one ball. The youngest ones can play in

flat soled athletic shoes and shin guards, shorts and a t-shirt. As the years go by, though, the players grow through shoes and shin guards and maybe warm-ups and rain gear too.

Your organization can help parents by providing information about gear. Although it's nice to have top of the line equipment, the youngest players certainly don't need it: a good pair of athletic shoes or cleats that fit right and a pair of shin guards that fit right, and they're done.

The organization can also do good public service by instituting a recycling program for soccer shoes and shin guards – both of which kids grow out of at a sometimes astonishing rate. People can bring outgrown gear to a certain spot, perhaps a bench or pavilion or bleachers at the local fields, and leave them. Those who need them can pick them up there.

All those lonely cleats and shin guards that are lying around in attics, entryways, and back hallways would rather be playing. ***Let's recycle!***

11. Make pickup soccer part of your culture

In most other places in the world, pickup soccer is a way of life, an essential part of the local soccer culture, a nursery for great talent. In parking lots and alleys, on beaches, in the park, behind a school – there are spontaneous games going on all the time.

Pickup games are where players polish their techniques, learn to think fast and outplay their opponents, fight for the ball, dream, overcome obstacles, use their imaginations, establish friendships and gain will power and force.

In most places in America, our youth soccer culture is, unfortunately, way too organized. In most settings, kids always or almost always play soccer in a 'controlled environment': a formal practice setting. They come to a field at six o'clock on Tuesday and Thursday nights, do soccer activities and play soccer for an hour or so, then drive home. On Saturday, they play in their weekly game for about half an hour, then drive home. In the best case, the players are stimulated and challenged at practices by an enthusiastic and upbeat soccer teacher: they play real soccer activities vigorously, and they run and think and answer questions presented by the coach – or by the games themselves. In the worst case, the players are put through boring, unrealistic exercises by an untrained coach who stifles creativity and imagination by always telling them what to do and, in effect, wastes their time. The results of the latter situation are kids who we see sitting on their ball before practice (the obvious escapes them!); kids who play, in practices and in games, without real alertness or fantasy or childlike joy; kids who think and act slowly on the field.

Coaches can get pickup games going in a number of ways:
- If you practice once a week, devote 30 minutes of every other week's practice to a pickup game. Don't coach during the game: assign two captains – who change through the weeks – to choose teams, and then let the kids play. No interventions.
- If you have two practices a week, use one of them as a tournament day. After a brief warmup, have four captains choose teams and then have a 3 v 3 or 4 v 4 tournament. You could even name the teams for countries (tonight, Ghana, Mexico, Japan, and Denmark) and have a small World Cup.
- In the summer, make it known that there will be pickup games at the town's practice field or in a park or behind a school on Tuesday and Thursday evenings and on Sunday afternoons. Then work out a schedule so that someone from the organization is there to get the ball rolling – not to coach or intrude, just to throw down some sweatshirts to make goals and to say, "I'll play with the team in light shirts." Then aunts and nephews, fathers and daughters, soccer moms, two new coaches, a guy who finished the D Course last month, and the organization's treasurer can get going!
- How about small pickup games for parents on the nights their kids are practicing, for friendship, fitness, and enjoyment?

♦ Encourage your own children and the players on your team to play pickup games at school during recess, on weekends, on the beach, while they wait for a ride home from school, all the time, everywhere.

Ironically, some coaches may think that pickup soccer games are frivolous, beside the point, a luxury. "Well, I'd like to see them playing pickup during practice, but I've got too much to cover. And if they're going to get together to play, they should be organized, and the session should be structured, so that they get a lot out of it." Good practices are vital for a player's development, sure, but so are free, exuberant pickup games. Trust the game to teach the kids! Painters need to work on the canvas and see what emerges, guitarists need to move around those frets and listen to what they hear, soccer players need to play hour after hour of free soccer.

After all, if you asked your players at the beginning of any practice, *"What would you most like to do tonight?"*, you know what they'd say.

Chapter Five

11 Suggestions for Practices

An enjoyable and productive practice session is a wonderful occasion for both players and coaches. There are some random aspects to most practices, those elements that are uncontrollable or unpredictable: the weather, the condition of the field, the fact that this evening everybody is "on", really into it (or not).

Almost all good practices, though, are no accident – they are the result of good planning and leadership, and they reflect a multitude of good habits and effective methods. An excellent, experienced coach can enhance everything about practice by relying on a solid grasp of all the 'tricks of the trade' and by creating a positive psychological climate. On the other hand, a practice that is poorly planned or that is afflicted with lots of inefficiencies will unravel fast.

Before getting into specific suggestions and the 'nuts and bolts' of practice management, a few words about your outlook and approach at practice. Soccer practices (and games) should be organized to serve the kids in question: they should be age-appropriate environments. Every single child is different from every other child in many profound and mysterious ways, but for our purposes as soccer leaders or coaches, it is necessary to generalize as we organize practice activities or games.

To help players as effectively as possible, we as coaches should first consider some variables: the age and experience and attitude of the players and our own background and experience in soccer. There are, as one would expect, usually consistent relationships between the age of the players and the experience of the coach. For example, most U8 teams have less experienced coaches, and most U14 teams have more experienced coaches, most of whom have played soccer themselves.

Practices should have a different feel and climate and objective every step of the way, as the years go by. And the role and outlook of the leader or coach should be different every step of the way, too, as the years pass.

In general terms, here is an expression of how the practice environment and the role and presence of the coach might be effectively connected. 'In general terms' means that there are exceptions: the excellent, precocious U12 club team; the team of 'recreational' U14's, some of whom are just beginning to play soccer, etc. If you find yourself in an extraordinary situation, then you must, of course, modify your presentation. But for the great majority of us coaching 'regular' teams, this expression or outline will serve as a guide:

For U6 and U8 Players

The big words are FUN, SIMPLICITY, and FREEDOM – both at practice and in games. The practice environment should resemble as much as possible a school playground or 'the street'; the activity leaders – as opposed to coaches – should be as unobtrusive as possible, intervening only to organize activities and to offer positive comments. Talk from the activity leader is at an absolute minimum! Everything is on the kids' terms: imagination, creativity and trial and error are encouraged. These years are for movement and for developing the central nervous system: agility, balance, and coordination, "getting good on the feet and with the feet". Now soccer is just playing with the ball, as the Swedes say, becoming "friends with the ball". We should present lots of simple activities to help the kids learn how to move the ball, to guide it, to kick it accurately. And some small, visually simple games: 2 v 2 or 3 v 3 or 4 v 4. Practice for the kids is 30 to 60 minutes of running, standing, chasing, kicking, sometimes more or less purposeful, sometimes fanciful, always child-like. No big agenda!

The best title for the adult in question here is "Activity Leader": from the leader: enthusiasm, positive vibrations, sound organization, patience, restraint, and humor.

The big objective here is to monitor space and time: to organize little 'soccer environments' that are not too big or too small and to keep a steady stream of stimulating soccer activities coming.

This stage calls for tremendous restraint on the part of the Activity Leader, who will probably wonder, at least subconsciously, if she or he is doing enough, "justifying their position", so to speak. Be assured: the less you do, the better. Talk as little as possible and let the games stimulate and teach the kids.

For U10 and U12 Players

Big words are still FUN and SIMPLICITY and FREEDOM, as the kids continue their explorations and discoveries and, we hope, increase their fascination with and love of the game. Soccer should still be about fantasy and dreaming and 'romance' – as opposed to practicality or some result or outcome that we desire. Just playing, a pleasure, a nice leisure time activity, and, sure, inherently, learning. Lots of technical repetition, becoming better 'friends with the ball', more movement and refinement of motions, coordination, control of the body. This is the vital time for technical development: mastering the ball, stabilizing movements, refining the central nervous system, gaining skill and flair. More emphasis now on communication, on using their bodies to protect or win the ball, on getting a feel for the game and its situations and possibilities.

The best title for the adult at this stage is "Soccer Teacher". From the Teacher: the same enthusiasm and positive spirit as ever, and a keen organizational sense. Plenty of stimulating and challenging games, focused particularly on technical development. Since these are critical years for learning, coaches should teach constantly throughout practices: technical pointers and tactical suggestions and principles. At the same time, coaches here should not be anxious about what they don't know; they should trust the game itself to teach. As long as the kids are playing challenging, realistic soccer activities, everything is fine. If you're coaching at this level, and you don't know soccer that well, you can prepare some brief lessons ahead of time: these two technical pointers during the shooting exercise and those two tactical pointers during the 4 v 4 games. Then, during those activities, stop the action, express those ideas (or demonstrate them, even better), and get the kids playing again right away. Don't let your inability to analyze techniques or tactical situations slow you down: you can bring plenty to practice with brief but sound preparation.

For U14 and U16 Players

Kids playing at these levels are generally experienced and more committed and in a competitive environment. FUN is still the central word and the most important consideration, but there are other important ideas, too. Now practice should be a learning environment that is filled with intense technical and tactical challenges and physical demands. Practices should call for concentration and focus and should help the players learn how to apply their skills in fast, realistic activities. The players should be aiming now to master all the techniques, 'read the game' astutely and make consistently good tactical decisions, and play with speed, strength, and composure.

Here, though, a note of caution. The kids now, if not toward the end of the previous stage, Stage Two, may not be as cooperative, receptive, or responsive as they were in the past or will be in the future. They may be at this age, as a matter of fact, uninterested, lethargic, or provocative – or a mystifying, frustrating combination of those and other qualities. Some may push your buttons, some may be more interested in small talk and giggling than in practicing, some may use sharp language. So here, as everywhere, you have to focus on the players first, then the soccer. With as much patience and humor as you can muster, express your expectations for practices – respect, focus, and good will – and try to make the duration of practice as enjoyable and interesting and challenging as possible. If the kids are disruptive, just put them aside, calmly, and carry on with the ones who came to play. If they are really out of line, perhaps a short talk with their parents after practice is called for. That should in no way be threatening: just a clarification of expectations and a request for better cooperation.

From the coach, or 'trainer': as always, enthusiasm and positive spirit and lots of encouragement to the players. At this level, though, more is required: solid knowledge of techniques and tactics, a sound grasp of coaching methodology, a keen ability to analyze, and maximum efficiency in terms of organization. Strong communication skills are vital, and the ability to demonstrate is important.

Some more thoughts about these priorities:
The most important activity for young soccer players is to play soccer. If an adult coach is going to gather kids at a soccer practice and organize something other than a pure soccer game, she or he should have a good reason for doing that. If the activities that the coach plans are not as valuable and productive and enjoyable as simply playing a soccer game, the coach should question herself or himself. If a coach isolates a technique and organizes an enjoyable activity to help the players to get better at that skill, and she or he does so efficiently and effectively, that's a valid objective. A brisk tactical lesson followed by an activity to help the players become more acute, perceptive observers and more alert, dynamic decision makers is a valid objective. Running laps, listening to long-winded commentaries about last Saturday's game, static and unrealistic 'drills': these are truly a waste of valuable time.

The most incisive way to express these objectives is to say: For the youngest players, techniques; for the middle players, more technical practice and awareness and perception and dynamism; for the older (U14 and up) players, learning to control the game and win the game.

As the basis: technique! Over and over, from sport to sport, coaches assert the primary importance of technique. In February of 2004, Oscar Robertson, one of the greatest basketball players of all time wrote a provocative -and, given the results at the 2004 summer Olympic Games' basketball competition, prescient - column in The New York Times. His contention was that basketball players these days are not mastering fundamentals and becoming complete players. He wrote:

"Players today are bigger, faster, stronger and more agile. But many of them can't dribble, can't shoot from outside, can't create shots off the dribble, can't guard anyone and are lost without the ball. Or even with it."

Jay Bilas asserted many of the same points in an article about basketball for ESPN: he regretted that as 'coaching' has become more prominent, 'teaching' of fundamentals has slipped, and he mentioned the short term gratification of coaches and specialization among young players as two reasons for the diminishing of skills.

Speaking about the Seattle Mariners' star Ichiro Suzuki, an opposing coach once said, *"They idolize technique and skill in Japan more than Americans do. How you do something is paramount in Japan. Here, it's more about achieving the numbers. Power is the American way."*

And one of the world's greatest soccer coaches, the Brazilian Carlos Alberto Parreiro, once said, in an interview in <u>World Soccer</u>, *"Soccer's greatest commodity is technique. Football, fortunately, is not a sport of velocity and strength; it should be based on technique, creativity, and even some artistic quality. Speed and power are important elements but they are not the foundations"*.

A few more points:
- Many coaches try to do too much, too fast, too soon. Kids need time to explore, to learn, to absorb, to stabilize; coaches should not rush them. (They also need time simply to have fun and enjoy being kids in a kids' world!) Some coaches feel anxiety or pressure for one reason or another ("These parents want results!", "I've only got a year, and I've got to teach them everything!", "I've only got a year, and – I must admit it – <u>I</u> want to win!", etc., etc.), and their leading or coaching can get distorted. Soccer is a simple game that relies on refined skills. The first priority must be to develop those skills.
- At practice, organize the time and space impeccably, but don't try to organize or control the playing itself, beyond

offering a few ideas about tactics. Trial and error, plenty of mistakes, lots of experimentation, freedom, and fantasy are all good. Mistakes help players to learn!

The simple fact is that in most other places in the world, kids learn to play soccer just by playing. Of course, they generally play many more hours than American kids do, but coaches should never forget this central truth: playing soccer is the best way to get good at soccer. Dribbling the ball, losing it, bumping that kid off the ball with my shoulder, taking it back, passing, sprinting, here comes the ball, I think I'll use that move I saw Ronaldo do, whooeee! *That's right!*

Here are eleven suggestions for practices:

1. Make a plan

No practice ever goes exactly as it was designed: there are just too many variables and unpredictable possibilities. Goals have to be moved, or a conversation before practice with a parent goes for a few extra minutes, so the beginning of practice is a little late. The players are really into the second activity of the session, so you let it go 10 extra minutes. There is a slight injury; the weather is very warm, so you give extra water breaks; one of the players has a suggestion about a set play at one of your breaks, so you take a few minutes to discuss that with the team. The list of factors that may change your exact practice design is endless.

Nevertheless, it is vital to make a brief plan before each practice: nothing particularly long or detailed, just a clear, brief outline of what you intend to do. You can write your plan out on a 3 x 5 card, a piece of notebook paper, or on a pre-designed sheet that you print out, from your computer. It's a good idea to put estimated times next to your activities, to keep you on track. For example, outlines might look like these:

For a U8 practice:

6:00 to 6:10	Dribbling and turning.
6:10 to 6:20	Targets.
6:20 to 6:25	Water, relaxing.

6:25 to 6:40	2 v 2 tournament.
6:40 to 6:45	Move cones, get organized; the kids are one-touch passing.
6:45 to 7:00	4 v 4 game, subs changing on the fly.

For a U14 practice:

6:00 to 6:10	4 v 1 keepaway.
6:10 to 6:25	2 v 1 plus goalkeeper tournament.
6:25 to 6:35	Water – and talk about and set up how we're going to defend corner kicks.
6:35 to 6:55	4 v 2 games: emphasis on techniques of receiving and 'opening' the game.
6:55 to 7:00	Organizing, talk.
7:00 to 7:25	8 v 8 game: two 10 minute halves with a five minute half time.
7:25 to 7:30	Cooldown.

Those two hypothetical outlines indicate a number of principles for practices:

- It's important to start with a ball right away. That's what the players want – <u>not</u> to run around the field or to review last Saturday's game! - so give it to them.
- For the younger players – U6 and U8 – the first activities are "one player, one ball": repetitive, isolated technical stuff. Lots of touches, lots of ball contacts.
- For the older kids – U10 and older – keepaway is a great way to start: it gets the players focused, it's mildly competitive, it involves several techniques, and it's a simple 'warming' tactical situation.
- The younger kids spend one quarter or one third of their time on isolated technical stuff; then they apply those techniques in small games. The older kids get into the games – with their inherent contention and confrontations – more quickly.
- We play as much as possible, talk just a little.
- Coaches must get good at math, to assure that no player is sitting or standing around. If we have one 'extra' player,

then one of our 3 v 1's becomes a 4 v 1, or a 'circulating' player is juggling, ready to change with a keepaway player as we call her in. If we have one fewer player than we figured, then a 4 v 2 becomes a 4 v 1, or we join in for a few minutes, etc.

2. Listen to and watch the players carefully

Coaches should use their senses as keenly as possible. Tune into the kids as soon as practice begins.

In the first few minutes, as they are warming up or beginning the first activity, get close to them and concentrate on sound; you can look away from them or even close your eyes. The kinds of sounds you hear will give you a good idea about their moods and energy levels. Sometimes there is animated talk everywhere, laughter, the sound of lots of moving feet; other times there is hardly any talk, and the atmosphere is subdued. A strange reality is that too often the kids are animated and noisy before practice, but as soon as practice starts, they get quiet. A good practice should be noisy (their noise, not ours!): animated, energized, spirited. Careful listening at the beginning of the session sometimes tells us that we have to get some energy into the air, clap our hands, get them going.

As the practice goes on, listen to their breathing, the sound of their feet on the ball, how noisy the running is, what they're saying as activities go on. Good coaches ask their players a lot of questions; they don't just make statements. Then they listen carefully to what the players say, both to show respect for the player and to evaluate the richness of the reply. This particular dynamic is really important if we want the kids to become good players: ask them questions, stimulate them, provoke them – then listen. Over the years, they have to come up with 'answers' to countless situations, and this conversational model, which relies on acute listening skills from them and from us, is central to the process. The kids will, of course, be more inclined to listen if our questions and comments are clear, brief, and to the point.

Just as we should listen carefully to the kids, we should watch them, too. Often we are so preoccupied by our practice plan and all that we want to accomplish that we don't regard the players as we should. Especially at the beginning of practice, watching intently can give us a lot of good information, and it can enable us to help the players more effectively. As your U10's are warming up by dribbling their balls around in a small area, you're watching and shouting:

"Good, Keisha, the ball is really staying with you tonight!"
"Arms up, head up, Alice, that's it!"
"Hey, everybody, keep your shoulders relaxed. Yes, better!"

3. Invest in a little gear

There is no need to buy a lot of clothing or equipment, but picking up a few items will help you both to look more authoritative and to organize your practice activities more effectively.

On you:
* A soccer shirt – t-shirt or polo shirt or soccer jersey. Perhaps your town or club provides this.
* Sweatpants or warmup pants or soccer shorts.
* Flat soled athletic shoes or cleats or running shoes (but it's not so easy to play soccer or demonstrate techniques in shoes with raised heels).
* No sunglasses. It's important that the players are able to see your eyes.

With you, in a small training bag (and the expectation is that many of these items would be provided by your town or club):
* First aid kit and sunscreen (for you and players who may have forgotten theirs, particularly for mid-day games or tournament days where you face prolonged exposure to the sun).
* Enough pinnies of two different colors so that you can split your squad into thirds: pinnie number one, pinnie number two, no pinnies.
* 16 or 20 small disc cones.
* 10 or 12 nine inch standing cones.

- A ball pump.
- A small cooler with ice and plastic bags.
- Notebook and pens.

And maybe with you:
- 10 or 12 large disc cones.
- A dry erase or magnetic coach's clipboard.
- A set of 'coaching sticks' – good for making fitness courses or to use as goals.
- A set of 'Dutch gates' – good for dribbling or passing exercises or to use as small goals.
- A few mini-balls. These are really valuable, especially for the younger kids. You an keep them circulating during warmup and 'isolated technical activities' time; you can play with them for a few minutes in your 4 v 4 games today. Or you can have one available so that the 'extra' player (you're playing two games of 4 v 2 and you have 13 players at practice, for example) can juggle it as she or he waits to rotate into one of the games.

The more we can create a soccer-like environment, the better, and the way we look and the gear we have available can help a lot. Towns and clubs and community centers are creating, as the years go by, soccer-specific spaces, with chalked out soccer fields, goals of different sizes, kickboards, kickbacks, or two-sided goals. That's excellent. Still, many of us have to practice on what is primarily a football field or a baseball field or on a grassy space in the midst of asphalt basketball courts. If we're in a New York Power t-shirt or a Boca jersey or an AC Milan warmup top, and we've made some nice 4 v 4 fields with discs and cones, we are creating a soccer environment.

4. Every player should have a ball at practice

Encourage all the kids to bring a ball. If they don't have one at the moment, perhaps they can ask for one on their birthday or at Hanukkah or Christmas. It's not a bad idea to bring along an extra ball or two to practice yourself.

Especially for the younger players, the higher the number of ball contacts they get at each practice, the better. A one ball per player ratio maximizes the number of activities you can plan, and part of each practice should be time for every player to dribble or juggle her or his ball – for improved control, flair, and confidence.

Get in the habit of using all the balls all the time, too. That means that if you are playing, for example, a 5 v 2 keepaway game, have the players set up their balls around the perimeter of the play space, two or three yards off the lines. That way, if the ball in play is knocked way out of bounds, the players can get another ball back in play quickly.

5. Think about your coaching position

Where you stand during practice is important. Here are some guidelines:

- At the beginning of practice, when you're gathering every one to explain, briefly, the shape of the practice or to start the first activity, stand still – and ask the players to stand still in front of you. With the very youngest players, you may want to squat down or go down on one knee. It's best to have the players in front of you, close, in a semi-circle: you can see all of them, and they can see you and hear you.
- Unless you are going into a grid – a playing area – to talk or 'make a picture', stand outside the lines. Coach on the outside, looking in. If you have to set up multiple grids, stay on the move: circulate among them to offer encouragement, observe and make coaching points.
- At water breaks, have the kids dribble all the balls to you, where they can leave them in a cluster. Then, as they drink water, you can check your practice plan, re-arrange discs or cones, and prepare for the next activity. The balls will act as a magnet: the kids will gravitate back to you, and you can give the next directions.
- Don't be a ball chaser: if shots miss the goal or roll or fly out of a grid, let the kids retrieve them. It's a positive impulse to want to be helpful, but your role is to organize, observe, lead, or coach.

- Another "don't": Don't become the 'counter' of a game or activity – the one who counts successful consecutive passes, or goals, etc. Let the players do that. You may have to assign a 'counter' at first or assign a captain for each team, but the kids will get the hang of that soon and quickly start to appoint themselves. On a practical level, if you're the counter, then you're pinned down at that grid or field until the game ends. The most important consideration, though, is that you want the players to be responsible for as much as possible. Let them do the counting so that you can stay on the move and concentrate on the big picture.
- During the time of practice that the kids are scrimmaging, if you're not playing with them or refereeing the game, take up various positions: at midfield, in one goal or the other from time to time, on the field. If you do come on to the field, be sure that you have a different colored shirt than that of either team. Staying on the move a little enables you to have different perspectives, to get around to talk with all the players, and to feel the climate all over the field.

6. Get feedback from the games and activities you organize

Whatever your level of experience or expertise, once you've organized activities or small sided games at your practice, watch them and listen to them carefully for valuable feeback.

If you see the kids moving dynamically and their voices are up and they're laughing, that's a good sign. If the kids seem lethargic, slow, static, and the game is quiet, then think about how effective or desirable the game in fact is. It may be just one of those nights, but maybe the kids don't like that game.

Sometimes the players will tell you directly, or indirectly, that they either like or dislike a particular game: that's helpful. Otherwise, you have to discern for yourself how effective and popular activities are, and decide whether to keep using them or not.

Of course, the players may also like certain games that you don't like or consider valuable. That's a judgment call. If you are resourceful and organize consistently stimulating practices, that shouldn't be an issue.

One piece of feedback is particularly helpful: the scores of the small games the kids are playing. To motivate and stimulate the players and to put them as often as possible in situations where it's important to outplay their opponents and <u>win</u>, scoring the small games in your practices is important. You can either limit the time ("OK, guys, we'll play five minutes – and let's really go – and then we'll take a break!") or play to a certain number of goals.

A good number is three goals. Let's say that you've organized 2 v 1 plus keepers or 2 v 2 or 3 v 3 games at practice. If you play to three goals, then change the teams, there are a number of positive outcomes:
- Playing to three is quick – the kids have to be sharp, or the game is over before they've gotten to grips with it. Urgency is in the air.
- If my pals and I are down 1 to 2 in a 3 v 3 game, our attitude is still: "We can win!"
- Pairs or teams are re-constructed constantly, which is a desirable practice dynamic.

Check continually on the scores of these games: then you can change game environments to maximize motivation and challenge. If goals are not coming, move the cones and make the goals bigger; if the teams are getting to three really fast, shrink the size of the goals. Making the field bigger or smaller will generally lead to more scoring, or less.

7. Get good at managing space

Making 'grids' – play spaces – that are the right size for your practice activities is really important. If you set up a game of keepaway (3v 1, 4 v 1, 5 v 2, etc.) and make the space too big, then the defenders will be de-motivated ("How the heck am I even going to get near the ball?"), and the passers will be de-motivated, too ("This is too easy!"). If you make the space too small, the defenders will also be de-motivated ("Man, all I have to do is move a little and stick out my leg and I get the ball."), and the passers, too. ("How can we string together passes in this tiny space?") Get the space right and the defenders will have to hustle and fight, and the passers will have to be sharp.

It won't take you long to get to know your team and its general ability level, and so you'll be able to plan pretty closely how large to make your spaces. It's amazing what a difference a yard or two makes - in the length or width of the grid or in the size of the goal. The key is to insure that every activity in your practice is as motivating and challenging and enjoyable as possible.

8. Get good at managing time

The most important 'managing' that we do at practice is to stimulate and motivate the players, to create an emotional environment where they can have fun, try things out, learn, develop as players and human beings. In trying to create that environment, how we manage space and time are central to success.

As for time:
   - Always start your practice right on time. Get to the practice site early, check the field and the goals for safety, lay out your gear – pinnies and cones. Set up the space or spaces for the first activity, then review your plan quickly and take a moment to look around, clear your mind, relax. Greet the kids and their parents as they arrive, then start right on time. If you're missing kids, start anyway: that will encourage promptness, and you want practice to be as long as it's supposed to be. In your pre-season meeting with the parents, ask them to bring the kids to practice early enough so that they can have their shoes on and be ready to start right on time.
   - Wear a watch and keep looking at it. Refer to your practice plan from time to time to be sure that you're on time.
   - Talk as little as possible! This takes practice, ironically. It's harder to talk a little than to talk a lot. Our talking shrinks practice time.
   - Think ahead, so that as one activity ends, you can move

quickly to set up the cones to mark out the next one. As you're organizing the cones, the kids can be having a period of 'active rest': one touch passing, juggling, slow speed dribbling and turning, etc. that makes productive use of transitional time.

+ On the other hand, sometimes it's valuable to give kids periods of absolute relaxation: social time. That could be at three five-minute water breaks during practice. Let them catch up on news, social stuff, get their conversation jones filled - then ask for focus and concentration when you resume. (Think U14 girls.)

+ At the U10 and older levels, try to get across to the kids: let's play as much as we can during practice! Tell them: I'll schedule in some water breaks and periods of active rest and maybe some social time, but the rest of the time, let's play with focus and lots of energy!

+ Times, for practices:
    U6: 30 to 40 minutes.
    U8: 60 minutes.
    U10: 75 minutes.
    U12 and on: 90 minutes.

It is questionable whether a team should ever practice for more than 90 minutes. There may be a reason to practice more: for example, your U14 club team practices once a week, and the kids are already driving up to an hour to get to the practice site. In that case, one two hour practice might be reasonable. In physical and mental and psychological terms, though, 90 minutes is a long time.

There's another reason why 90 minutes should be long enough. Kids these days have complex lives, and family households, their lives' contexts, have complex dynamics. Youth coaches must always keep in mind that soccer is played in a cultural, family context. From a mother's point of view, for example, if your 11 year old daughter has practice from 6:00 to 7:30 tonight, that may occupy you and disrupt the supper schedules of your eight year old son and your husband – as well as that of your daughter and you.

One and a half hours is enough of a commitment to ask of a player <u>and</u> her or his household. High school players especially, who have homework, other interests (one would hope), families who like to see them, and often jobs and other pressures like college applications, should not practice more than 90 minutes.

More is not necessarily better.

For U12 and older kids, don't plan longer, more physically grueling practices. Plan brisk, stimulating, efficient 60 to 90 minute practices – which will keep the kids fresh. They'll feel better – and so will the other members of their families.
End practice right on time. The kids need to get home to eat, do homework, and relax, and there are always a million things to do around the house for the parents. In your pre-season parents' meeting, ask parents to be prompt about pickup after practice – and then be firm about that request. After a long day of work and an hour and a half of coaching, volunteered, it's not fair to you and your assistant (or the week's parent-assistant) to be kept waiting, with a player, for a tardy parent.

9. Be sure that another adult is present at your practice

If you're lucky enough to have an assistant, because your town or club system is well organized and resourceful, that's good. But most youth coaches are on their own. It's important to have another adult with you.

- In case of injury, they can look after the injured player as you watch over the team – or vice versa.
- It's preferable to have two adults present at the beginning and end of practice for the peace of mind of the players and parents.

If you don't have an assistant, you can circulate a calendar at your pre-season meeting and ask parents to sign up for one week. There is no need for them to do anything other than be present, from the beginning of practice until the last child is picked up. They can sit in their car and read <u>Love Medicine</u> or <u>The Brothers Karamazov</u>. They can also support you by encouraging the kids, helping you move cones, going after those two balls that missed the goal. Who knows: they may get interested and turn out to be a valuable assistant.

10. Use names, be positive

Kids need encouragement, they appreciate positive recognition, they like the sensation of success. There's something powerful about using their names: it shows respect, friendliness, regard. Try to speak to each player by name twice during each practice; they'll appreciate the connection and the recognition.

Try to keep all your expressions positive, too. Be sure that any criticisms are constructive and fair and accurate. A youth coach's language should never be angry, blameful, or harsh – and profanity is out of the question.

Try to keep your tone of voice and body language positive, too: kids are intuitive, and they pick up on all that right away.

11. Enjoy Nature!

Most of us work inside, under cover, in an environment that is artificially warmer or colder than that outside. Then we come to practice or a game, and the climate and weather and ground conditions are … just what Mother Nature wants them to be. Since we're so often insulated from the variations and extremes of our environment, conditions can seem to be an impediment or a negative element of the game. But getting to grips with natural conditions is stimulating and exhilarating, a genuine challenge. One of the most intriguing aspects of soccer is how natural conditions affect play, and Nature can sometimes complicate our practice plans or our game days.

If you live in Texas, you have to deal, during some months, with unrelenting heat; if you're from Maine, then your Fall season will require you to adjust to cold, maybe snow, maybe frost covered fields. Some places get big rainfalls, some are windy all the time, some confront the players with the challenge of playing in thin air – or smoggy air.

94

You can help the kids adjust to and neutralize these challenging aspects. Suggest that they:

- In the cold, warm up well, stay warm on the sidelines, wear gloves on the field.
- In the heat, slow down, drink plenty of water, and be very alert to the signs of heat exhaustion.
- In the wind, choose to go with it in the first half (it may change), keep the ball on the ground, be aware of how the wind will hold some balls up and alter the flight of others.
- In the rain, be careful of footing, watch for puddles, which will kill the ball, and expect passes and shots to skip off the wet grass.

The players can get used to all these adjustments at practices.

For sure, the conditions that Nature blows at us or drops on us can be tough or challenging – but we should do our best to think of them always in a positive light – and encourage our players to do the same. Encountering the natural world is always wonderful. Remember:

"Nature never wears a mean appearance."
Ralph Waldo Emerson

Chapter Six

11 Concepts to Impart to Young Players

Over the years, developing soccer players will confront hundreds of ideas, notions, questions, commands, assertions, musings, and principles as they learn how to play the game. Some of these abstractions and concepts will deal with techniques, some with tactics, others with physical fitness or with their psychological approach to the game.

For example: a smiling coach delivers a suggestion about shooting technique to her U10 team and then offers an impeccable demonstration of what she means. A dynamic young coach makes some comments about wing play and attacking the goal and then asks the kids to react to his thoughts. A coach who really knows her stuff picks up a team, and the players quickly realize that she prefers to ask them questions rather than tell them what to do. And on and on. Week after week, if they're lucky, kids will pick up information, inspiration, and stimulation, and they'll become clever, sharp players.

One of our great challenges as coaches is to impart this information appropriately, both in terms of substance and in the manner of our presentation. It's easy to miss the mark here, by talking too much, by using abstract terms when the kids need concrete ones, by introducing concepts too early, or going too fast. All kids and all teams are different, but there are some sensible generalities to guide us as we try to influence the players' thinking.

For the younger kids, U6's and U8's, playing is most important: running, guiding the ball, kicking, chasing, checking things out. Players at these ages generally have a limited ability to absorb abstract ideas about soccer (or about anything else). This has nothing to do with inherent intelligence. It's just that, at their young ages, kids are concrete thinkers who live in the here and now. It's best to make simple statements to these kids, one point at a time, about techniques. Simple, short, and as concrete as possible. Here, more than ever, we should remember that a picture is worth a thousand words. For example, pair up your U8's and let them kick their ball back and forth at their partner's target for a few minutes, then stop them and ask them to look at you.

"Hey, guys, look!" Then you turn your foot sideways. Point to your ankle and jab your index finger against the inside of your foot, back by your ankle joint. "Here's where I kick it! Watch this. OK, go ahead, keep kicking!" Then they kick 50 or 60 more balls.

Then watch and listen to your team. It's likely that for a couple of years, it will be best to keep your comments and instructions at an absolute minimum. Organize them so that they can <u>play</u>, <u>do</u>, <u>feel</u>, <u>try</u>, and <u>act</u>.

Before you know it, they're U10 players (or you've inherited a U10 team); now comes the time for more 'coaching', more verbal interactions, more teaching, more ideas. It's still best to keep all our expressions short, specific, and concrete, but we can now assert some basic concepts, 'make pictures' of those concepts, and discuss them with our players. At U10, most kids are ready for a little conceptual talk and some abstraction, as long as we keep expressions short and simple (and remember why they come here!). And because of the nature of young kids and of the learning process, we should accept the fact that we're going to have to repeat ourselves patiently, over and over, as the players absorb these concepts and learn to convert them into habitual actions.

Simplicity! Clarity! Patience!

Here are eleven concepts to impart to your players. These ideas deal mostly with tactics and with attitudes more than with techniques or fitness, although there are some technical pointers among the "additional ideas". They are all simple and intuitive and self-evident: none of them is over the head of the average U10 player or is inaccessible to most U10 to U14 players. Some of them are so simple and self-evident, as a matter of fact, that the players may consciously or unconsciously think, as you introduce them, "Oh, come on, everybody knows that." Well, maybe everybody does know that, but the coach is probably going to have to repeat that concept about 50 more times.

One of the fascinating aspects of soccer – or any sport for that matter – is that it relies on such simple concepts and principles, and yet even the best players fail to remember them or fail to 'play by them' occasionally. With all due respect to these players, sometimes WUSA players give the ball away carelessly, MLS players don't contribute to defending as they should, national team players don't shoot when they have the chance.

So coaches have a lot of work to do!

The eleven concepts are presented here in the fewest words possible: as a one-liner or as a simple expression. After each concept come related ideas, expanded comments, additional thoughts.

Each of these concepts is simple, but all of them, considered as a group, together with the supplementary ideas, represent a tremendous amount for players to absorb. An ambitious – but realistic – objective is to impart all these concepts to the players in the five years between U10 and U14.

1. Keep the ball safe – protect the ball

Let's suggest to the players: "Once our team has won the ball, let's do everything we can to keep it. Our attitude should be: we won't let the opponent get the ball until we shoot it into his goal!".

Right from the start, at the U10 level at the latest, let's get the players thinking about protecting the ball individually if they're under pressure by getting between the ball and the challenging player and fighting to keep it.

We should also talk to our players about the critical difference between giving the ball away and losing it. If we just kick the ball aimlessly up the field and it goes to the other team, we've given it away. If we lose our concentration and the ball bounces off our foot out of bounds, we've given it away. If we make a careless square pass in midfield when there is no real pressure on us, we've given it away. On the other hand, if our winger tries to dribble past their wingback and gets bumped off the ball, if our center forward shoots on the turn and their keeper makes a nice save, or if our halfback tries to split their defensive line with a pass that is intercepted, then we've "lost the ball". For players U10 to U14, we should assert: it's never good to lose the ball, but let's see if we can avoid even giving it away. Then, of course, we must be patient when they continually lose the ball or give it away!

As the months and years go by, we should talk with our players about various tactical applications of this concept. For example: "We must never give the ball away (and, later, even lose the ball) in our own half. So be careful about dribbling or making square passes back there!". We should patiently, over time, explain the notions of safety and risk in the various areas of the field: our team should play safely in our own half; we must be willing to take some risks (shooting, clever passes, dribbling at people) near our opponent's goal.

This concept is as much a question of psychology as it is a question of tactics. If our players develop confidence and com-posure and train themselves to be alert and focused, we'll do much better at keeping the ball. Playing plenty of small-sided, pressured games will help the players gain the technical compe-tence that will lead to that combination of confidence and aware-ness; they have to get used to the fight, the struggle.

Let's take that issue of psychology one step further and consider for a moment how the psychology of the parents can affect the understanding of this concept by the players. If the parents on the sideline during the week's game are emotional or tense, they may also be yelling advice and instructions:
- "Shoot, Paula!"
- "Get it out of there! Boot it!"
- "Don't dribble! Pass it up the field!"
- And the all time classic – "Send it!"

The combination of emotional static in the air and bad advice will distract and unsettle the players; it will affect their emotional states and their judgments, and it will make it more difficult to calmly and effectively take care of the ball.

If the parents are relaxed (or trying to stay relaxed) and quiet and they are cheering for everyone, then the kids will be much more inclined to focus on the ball and on keeping it in the team.

There is one particular situation that deserves a lot of our attention when it comes to protecting the ball: the tendency of many young players to turn 'into pressure' when they have possession. Here's an image: the left halfback passes the ball up to the left wing, who - (incorrectly) facing back toward the halfback, instead of standing sideways on, open to the field - receives the ball with her right foot, settles the ball, and then, with the next touch, turns the ball toward and into the defender who has come up to challenge her. There is a 'thud' as two feet hit the ball at the same time; whose ball it is next is anybody's guess. That same movement – of a player turning toward trouble, in essence unwittingly 'looking for a fight', will be repeated many times all over the field during the game.

We have to help the players learn how to make space for themselves so that they can receive the ball better, get away from that defender, or roll or spin off her, so that they can then shoot or pass or dribble ahead.

2. Shoot every chance you get

You know how it is: your U10 team works the ball out of your own end with a couple of nice passes, and one of the kids dribbles the ball across the half field line, 30 yards from the opponent's goal. Suddenly, one of the fathers yells, "Shoot!"

Not quite yet!

On the other hand, your players get within shooting distance and make one pass too many and lose the ball, or they have an opening to shoot and instead try to dribble past one more defender and lose the ball. Either way – no goal.

We should say to the kids: Hey, be patient! You're all solid and clever, and as long as we dribble and pass intelligently, the ball is ours. Let's get close enough to their goal to score, then let's shoot! The key is: when we're close enough, let's finish the job.

That means that any time your players get near the opponent's goal, they must be alert and ready for action, light on their feet and balanced, expecting the ball to come their way. No more passing or dribbling now, just cool finishing. Your players, once they get near that net, must be single minded.

We can help our players to develop this aggressive attitude about shooting by stressing it as often as possible in our small games at practice. Whenever we play a 4 v 4 game, we can ask, when it ends, "How many of you took a shot or shots, and how many of you scored?"

3. Help your teammate with the ball

Soccer is a team game, and it's a passing game. Until your kids are in a position to put the ball into the net, the game is all about passing and receiving and dribbling and keeping the ball in the team.

Too many youth games are characterized by the player with the ball being active and almost everybody else on the team being passive. Of course, without support, the ball possessor won't be active for long! At the younger ages, it's not uncommon to see one player dribbling, and all her teammates just watching. Even at older ages, it's not as common as it should be to see players yelling to one another, making quick movements to offer help, obviously scheming and thinking ahead, thinking *"How can I help, how can I make some trouble here?"*

Let's assert to our players: *"When a teammate near you has the ball, try to be helpful. Take a position directly behind her or at an angle behind her if she's under pressure, or directly in front of her or at on angle in front of her if she's not under pressure. Use your voice and your body to communicate with her: she should be able to get a lot of information from your inflection and the urgency in your body, how you are relaxed or coiled, how you signal with your hands. Don't be passive! Make it clear that you want the ball, that you're ready to help, that she has a good option by getting the ball to you.".*

As the players get older, coaches can offer lots more tactical ideas about how players can help the ball possessor – and not necessarily by asking for a pass. Players 'off the ball' can open up space, can be decoys, can make defenders face choices that are awkward, like whether or not to cross over another defender (which defenders do not want to do, but which is tempting at this moment…).

The big principle that we can get to the players right away, though, and then refine over the years is: *"Let's get more players around the ball than they have. Then we'll use our skills and smarts to outplay them.".*

4. Learn to use your body to keep the ball and to win the ball

Soccer is a tough game played by strong people. Within a set of rules designed to keep the game fair and under control, players try to keep the ball or win the ball with all the speed and power that they have. Even the youngest players, who don't perhaps have all that much speed or power, try, without any real calculation, to play 'fast and strong'.

Some kids are more coordinated than others, quicker and more aggressive; and, of course, some kids are bigger than others. If you and I are U10 players, and I'm more agile than you, I weigh 15 pounds more than you, and I like the hurly burly of the game more than you, I'm probably going to outplay you, 'out-duel' you more often than not. Especially in youth soccer, there is often a disparity among the players in terms of their physical resources and their attitudes toward the tough clashing of bodies that the game requires. Some kids are rather small and not particularly coordinated, and by nature they are shy or hesitant; they are not aggressive or assertive. A classic question from youth coaches is, *"How can I help so and so or my team be more aggressive?"*

That's a nearly unanswerable question. If we set up a lot of small, pressured games, and we organize activities where the kids are fighting for the ball, week in and week out, year in and year out, the kids will generally get stronger and tougher. Some kids are not so set up for the rough and tumble, though, and they may have difficulty with all the bumping and contending. That's life. We should keep encouraging them, accept their attitudes, and keep helping them. This lack of aggressiveness is sometimes hard for a parent to accept – especially if that parent is the coach; they may think, particularly in our competitive, comparative culture, that it is some sort of negative reflection on them.

In any case, coaches should keep teaching and be patient. Under no circumstance should the coach ever question, privately or in a group, the courage or toughness of a child. Nothing constructive could come of such a question.

We should try to help all the kids get better on their feet: better balanced, stronger, more effective on and off the ball. By organizing lots of duels – 1 v 1's, 2 v 1's 2 v 2's, in small spaces, where there will be a lot of clashes and struggles, we create the environments where kids can learn how to use their bodies to keep possession of the ball or to win the ball back.

We have to keep reminding the kids that soccer is a fight. "The other team doesn't want you to play! They want the ball! They're going to attack you until they win it! Get ready!" Or, on the other hand, *"Hey, did you think they would just give it back to you? No way! You're going to have to fight as hard as they just did to take the ball from you. Get ready!"*

Now one of your players has the ball and is under pressure, perhaps pinned against a line or in a crowd in midfield. (These remarks are not intended for players who are <u>not</u> under pressure – that is, those who can get their bodies around and dribble at the defender.) You can help her by saying:
- "Quick – get your body between that opponent and the ball. Quick – here she comes!"
- "Now turn yourself sideways so that there's a line between the ball, your two feet, and her. Good!"
- "Spread your feet apart to 'make your body wide', and bend your knees. Don't get stuck to the ground – keep moving your feet and adjusting to her challenge."
- "Stay springy on your feet but be strong – she's going to bump you and use her legs to fight you in a moment."
- "Use the foot that is farthest away from her to touch the ball."
- "You can use your arm that is toward her to feel where she is and to keep her away from the ball – but you can't push her or hold her."
- "Use your shoulder! Keep her away from the ball by using your shoulder to block her away – get down low so that she

can't knock you off balance, or up and off the ball. How you use your shoulder is really important!"

- "Now – think about where she is. If she's ahead of you – that is, ahead of that line through the ball, your feet, and her – then there's a space behind you. If she's behind you, then there's a space ahead of you. As soon as she decides to challenge you in one direction or the other, 'spin' or 'roll' quickly with the ball and get away from her."

A reminder: please be patient! These several bullet points represent many weeks of patient teaching, one point at a time, by you; and several years of practice on the player's part.

Now let's turn the tables: your player's opponent has the ball against the line, or she just beat your player to it in midfield, or the two are running side by side, with the opponent in possession. Now you could say:

- "Keep your legs moving and keep them under you: don't reach or stretch for the ball. Get close to your opponent and use your legs first, then your upper body if you need to. As soon as she 'shows' you the ball, exposes the ball, reach in with a strong foot and take the ball."
- "Get low, come in hard, and try to get your shoulder in front of hers. That way, you can 'pry' the ball away from her."
- "If you bump into her – and you 're almost sure to – keep your legs moving. If you knock her a little off the ground or she stops moving her legs, you'll get the ball."

Here is a classic image from youth soccer: a group of U10 or U12 players is warming up or free dribbling, at the beginning of practice. They're dribbling around fluidly, turning sharply, making clever moves, looking really good. We're thinking, *"Wow, these kids are smooth; they really know how to play!"*

Then when the small games begin, those same kids give the ball away time and again by exposing it, they turn right into pressure, their stances are not strong, and they're constantly bumped off the ball. Their feet are rather slow, their legs are straight (not bent and coiled), and they hardly use their upper bodies.

This group of kids may be athletic and technically accomplished and show that they know soccer moves – but they clearly don't know how to use those moves and their bodies, how to act in the context of the game, how to <u>fight</u>.

A player's body is not just for controlling the ball: it's also for fighting against an opponent, with and without the ball. Let's help the players learn to do that as well as they can. The best way to learn this lesson – and most other soccer lessons – is to play small-sided games in compressed spaces, or to play a free-flowing pickup game.

If our team loses the ball, do what you can to win it back or to help our team to win it back. It's a whole lot more fun to play with the ball than without it! We should suggest to our team that, if we lose the ball, the faster that we win it back, the faster we can have that big fun.

That's not to suggest that we ask our players to charge after the ball thoughtlessly, to 'over-commit', to be too hasty as we try to win it. We can help our young players to learn to defend better with a few simple suggestions:

For the player nearest the ball when we lose it –
- "Get yourself between the ball and our goal. Let's call that 'goal side'."
- "Get down low and get as close to the ball possessor as you can. Go toward her as fast as you can, but stay under control. That is: "Close her down!" The big principle is that we want to meet our opponent as far from our goal as possible, never standing still, moving backwards only when we have to."
- "Stay on the balls of your feet with your knees bent and feet about shoulder width apart – and watch the ball carefully. Glance around quickly to size up the situation, then concentrate on the ball."
- "Now get ready! If the ball possessor tries to shoot or pass the ball, block it or knock it down; if she tries to dribble by you, wait for a moment when she gets a little separated from the ball, then tackle her with a strong 'block tackle'.

Get in low and block the ball with the inside of your foot –
or bump her off the ball with your shoulder."

*For the player or players close to the ball – but not confronting
the ball possessor -*

- ♦ "Keep communicating with your teammates, especially with
  the player who is 'pressing' the ball. You can tell that player
  who is closest to the ball, for example, that you 'have her
  covered' if she wants to tackle the ball possessor or you
  can ask her to "squeeze" the ball possessor against the
  sideline."
- ♦ "Do your best to provide "cover" for the player who is pressing the ball – to provide a second level of defense. Then
  you can step up and tackle the ball possessor if she
  happens to beat your pressing teammate, or you can block
  passes and shots. Stand close enough so that you're 'in
  the play' but not so close that a dribble or shot or pass goes
  past both your pressing friend and you. Position yourself
  on or close to a line between the ball and the goal, if possi
  ble."

  - These angles and distances for that 'covering'
    defender are flexible: they depend on the skill of
    the immediate opponent, where the ball is, the
    score, the placement of other opponents, etc.
- ♦ "At the same time that you're trying to help your friend who
  is pressing the ball or coming a little closer to other teammates who may need your help in a moment, you should
  try to blot out opposing players: get close enough to them
  so that if a pass comes their way, you're first to the ball – or
  a close second, close enough to put them under pressure
  immediately. (That's generally called "marking".) Get yourself 'goal side' of that immediate opponent and "ball side",
  too: shaded to whichever side of your opponent the ball is
  on."
- ♦ "The instant your team loses the ball, you must change
  your thinking. Instead of spreading out the 'making the field
  big', now it's about coming a little closer to your teammates
  and controlling as much space as you can. Instead of trying to move the ball ahead, now it's about trying to force the

other team to play the ball across the field or back – and then to give you the ball."

Defending will get more and more tactical as the years go by. Those of us involved with the youngest players should aim to help the kids with basic ideas about defending: how that player closest to the ball should act, how the players close to her should act. Those are complex issues, and they'll take up a lot of our time during the years the kids are U10 to U14 players.

6. Play with all you've got

This is questionable advice for us to give U6 or U8 players. They either play with all they've got, or they don't; their approach may change in the next minute; they may exhibit three levels of concentration within 10 minutes. Their attention wavers, their focus comes and goes, they're all action or out of gas. Who knows what they're thinking? Just let them run and move the ball and chase and have a blast.

But with the U10 kids we can start to say, gently: Hey, come on – when we're playing, let's really play! Then when we're taking a break, let's really take a break! If we're catching our breath, let's really catch our breath.

We may be able to guide the U12 players and the U14 players to show even more concentration and focus. One would hope so, but you never know; it all depends on the maturity, cognitive and psychological states, motivation, and chemical state of each player. That's a lot of variables, especially in the sometimes volatile years of pre-adolescence and adolescence.

It's good to remember that sometimes professional coaches are challenged to motivate their (experienced, big time, millionaire, famous) players to 'really play' when they're playing.

It's an excellent objective, though, for the kids to get into the habit of playing hard all the time. It will help their fitness, reduce the distance between the practice environment (often too soft) and the weekly game environment, and inspire their teammates.

They'll get more out of practice and perform more consistently in games.

We can help this process if we give the younger kids more frequent breaks (so that they can really relax), with social time or 'active rest', and if we gradually expand, over the months and years, the length of the play time when we're asking them to commit themselves.

Intense activity – complete relaxation: good!

And, of course, this attitude will have some fine carry-overs into the players' lives off the field: when they're studying Spanish verbs, they should really study Spanish verbs; when they're practicing the saxophone, they should really practice the saxophone; when they're cleaning up their room, they should really clean up their room.

7. Stay in the game

"Playing with all you've got" has to do with exertion and energy and motivation, often with physical commitment and bravery. "Staying in the game" is more about keeping the tactical mind active, staying 'in the moment', not 'switching off'. If kids are worrying about the mistake they just made – or think they just made, or they're anxiously wondering if their team can hang on to their one goal lead for the next 12 minutes, they're not 'in the game'.

We should encourage the kids to be constantly alert, to look around, to keep communicating with teammates, to anticipate. The Dutch have popularized a phenomenal notion about the game; that it has four "moments". Our team does not have possession of the ball, then there's a moment of transition as we gain the ball, then we have the ball, then there's a moment of transition as we lose the ball. Then the cycle starts once again. Our players have to learn to stay engaged and involved every step or every 'moment' of the way, always observing, evaluating, plotting, scheming, fantasizing, acting.

Two great expressions to get to the kids are:
- "Don't switch off!" (But then, easy, easy, stay cool when they do.)
- "What if...?" – as in "What if she shoots right now?" "What if Sean loses his grip on that kid?" "What if Carla passes to me?"

Some players are only lively when your team has the ball, some players are sharp only when the ball is near them, some kids show more intensity when the other team has the ball. We have to help them to stay in the game from start to finish.

We can also have more influence on the kids about this notion if our town or club stays with six or seven or eight-a-side soccer as long as possible: then the kids will always be closer to the ball, and the game, with all its possibilities, will come to them more often.

8. Try new stuff

Young players are constantly thinking – or half thinking – or sort of thinking or engaging in whatever process they use to decide on an action: Should I try that new dribbling move now? Is this a good time to use that new shoulder tackle we learned last week? Is this a chance for Jose and me to try a cross-over just outside the penalty area?

They'll never know if they don't try!

We should assert to the kids that practices are for learning and experimenting and repeating and getting confident – and then games are for trying stuff out, using skills, trying to outplay the other team. We should assure them by what we say and then, more importantly, by how we act during games (that is, we're calm, upbeat, unfazed), that they should feel free on Saturday.

The essence, pre-game: "Hey, girls, what a great day we have for a game! Now, have fun out there. Don't worry about mistakes. You all know what you're doing – but undoubtedly some things won't go right. No problem! Try things out!"

Of course, if the kids try crazy stuff – a fancy new dribbling move right in front of your goal, a cheeky pass across our goal mouth, etc. – we should talk with them. Otherwise, we should encourage them to play as freely as possible.

This concept can be a real challenge for some coaches. Many coaches are so obsessed with getting a positive result in the game that they want to minimize or <u>eliminate</u> risk and error; they want only safety and predictability. They're misunderstanding soccer, or they're about to distort it. Sure, we must play with common sense and security and regard for the principles of the game, but when the ball starts rolling, creativity and fantasy should prevail. Some coaches might say: we should only try in games what we've practiced. To a large extent, that's inherently true. But remember: every time Maradona dribbled by someone, every time Michelle Akers scored a goal, every time Paolo Maldini snatched the ball from a winger: that's all new!

Soccer is like jazz. There's a framework, an essential understanding among the players. Then the game or the music starts, and the players get ideas. Miles Davis bobs and weaves, Johan Cruyff leaves a defender wondering where he went, Cassandra Wilson interprets a lyric, Maren Meinert makes an outrageous no-look pass.

Famous players are famous because they try stuff.

Last: trying stuff out in the speed and pressure of a game will cause some mistakes, for sure. If negative reaction to those mistakes is constant and vociferous – from us or the parents – the players will be much less inclined to try new possibilities. We must stay positive and calm and composed, and we must ask the parents to do the same.

9. Be versatile

The modern game is fast and fluid and requires that all players are able to attack and defend. However, many players decide too early where they prefer to play on the field, and then certain of their functional capacities go underdeveloped.

We should encourage the kids to play all over the field and to want to play all over the field: left, center, and right; up, middle, and back; and, yes, in the goal. That way, they become all-round, two-way players, good with and without the ball, good at keeping it, good at getting it back. They understand the various functions and positions, they develop both feet, and they're much more resourceful for the rest of their playing days.

Here, too, our attitudes and approaches and those of the parents are crucial. If we base our practices on lots of small sided games and move our players around during the week's game, then the kids will learn to attack and defend and function in various parts of the field. So much the better if we can teach the players the techniques and tactics they'll encounter in the 'climates' around the field: how to shoot up front, to tackle all over the field, how to calculate safety and risk.

In this regard, it is important to keep in mind our big task: to help each player develop as an all-round soccer player. Many coaches slip into thinking just about the short term: they play that clever 11 year old only at center forward for a year or that 12 year old who is four inches taller than anyone else on the team only in the goal. So those two players have a diminished, one-dimensional year at a crucial period of their development.

We should discuss this issue with the parents of our players, too. They may assume that soccer is a game for specialists, and, of course, they would all like their child to be the top scorer. They may think that by moving around the field the kids may not learn any position 'well enough' — more irony.

It would be fantastic if all the players arrived at or hit the U15 or U16 level able to play all over the field with excellent techniques and sound tactical sense: confident, resourceful soccer athletes.

10. Play fair

Whoever made up the rules of soccer thought of everything. Imagine a soccer game where you <u>could</u> obstruct or push or hold opponents! They constructed a frame of behavior to enable strong, skillful players to compete with one another on a field where contention is constant and tough. The game they imagined is tough but civilized, logical but absolutely free, antagonistic but positive.

It's up to everyone who plays or enjoys soccer to keep it fair and right. Coaches must set an impeccable example of dignity and self-control and balance, and must demand the same of their players. A youth soccer game should be a positive setting, characterized by humor, friendly spirit, and good conduct. Youth soccer coaches should never think about teaching 'tricks' that bend the rules, or about gamesmanship or 'working' the referee.

Coaches should consistently demand of their players:

- ◆ Strict adherence to the rules – the spirit and letter of the law. Young players instinctively know what is fair; there are hardly ever 'real' fouls in a U8 or U10 game. As the kids get older (and bigger, faster, and more combative), it is their responsibility to learn the rules and to play by them.

- ◆ Acceptance of the authority and decisions of the referee – and an appreciation for how tough and, most of the time, thankless the job is.

- ◆ Respect for the beauty and spirit of soccer, for teammates and opponents, for coaches and referees and parents.

11. Play soccer all the time, everywhere!

- ◆ "What do you think would happen if you juggled for 15 minutes every day?"
- ◆ "Tennis balls are not only for tennis, you know."
- ◆ "I know what you mean; the ball does act differently on the beach."

- "I'm going to drop two sweatshirts on the ground over here. Tell me what you see."
- "What do you think walls <u>are</u> for?"
- "15 minutes of recess at school is a long time."
- "One of the reasons that birds and squirrels live in the park is so that they can watch people play soccer."
- "Hold it right there! I think that you forgot to put something in your backpack this morning!"

Chapter Seven

11 Warmups and Isolated Exercises

When the youngest players (U6) arrive at practice, get them buzzing around with their ball. Lots of movement, running, chasing, some target games, kicking around, then some minia-ture activities like 2 v 2. This should be considered "introduction" in many senses of the word: putting this new toy in front of them, getting them used to its movements and vitality, showing them a little athletic setting. Some of them will literally not be sure where they are, some will be so preoccupied with their own ball that they can't focus on anything else, some may want to spin around or roll in the grass or pretend to fly. Who can blame them?

These kids don't need to do what we would call warmup. They're always warm! They don't need to stretch or listen to us, either. They need the ball!

Some towns have the U6's play their weekly game as the second half of a 60 to 75 minute play-time after 30 minutes or so of practice. That's fine.

A brief U6 practice outline might look like this:

(Saturday morning)

9:00 to 9:10	Free dribbling, follow your partner, turning.
9:10 to 9:20	Tag and Targets.
9:20 to 9:35	2 v 2
9:35	Water and get organized.
9:45 to 10:15	Weekly game.

For the U8 players, a period of warmup activity and some isolated exercise, that is, unopposed technical stuff, is a good way to begin. A ball per player at first, to get lots of ball touches, lots of repetitive movements, and a gentle start. (U8's can get right into practice. U10's should do a little dynamic movement and stretching, and U12's and U14's should be sure to warm up and loosen up before they gear up the speed, dynamism, and competitiveness.) Then, for the U8's, quickly, more dynamic movement, speed, and contention: that all constitutes about a third of practice time. Then: miniature games and a scrimmage.

A U8 practice outline might be:

(Wednesday evening)

6:00 to 6:10	Free dribbling, quick feet, turning.
6:10 to 6:20	Gates and Targets.
6:20	Water.
6:25 to 6:45	3 v 3 tournament: three five-minute games.
6:45 to 7:00	5 v 5 game.

A great way to start U10, U12, or U14 practices is to play keepaway: lots of touches, good for focusing the soccer brain, gently competitive. Then a period of isolated exercises, some small games, and a scrimmage.

A U10 practice outline could be:

(Thursday evening)

6:00 to 6:10	Keepaway: 4 v 1 or 5 v 1 (depending on how many kids get to practice), in small rectangles; and dynamic movements.
6:10 to 6:20	Knockout, with two minutes of juggling at the end.
6:20 to 6:30	Water, and talk about and set up attacking on corner kicks.
6:30 to 6:50	3 v 1 plus 2 keepers.
6:50	Water.
6:55 to 7:15	6 v 6 game.

A possible U12 or U14 practice:

(Wednesday evening)

6:00 to 6:10	Keepaway – 4 v 1 or 5 v 1 in small rectangles, and dynamic movements.
6:10 to 6:25	1 v 1's in front of the goal.
6:25 to 6:35	Water, and talk about and show how to defend throw-ins.
6:35 to 6:55	4 v 2.
6:55	Water and get organized.
7:00 to 7:25	Game: two ten minute halves with a five minute half time.
7:25 to 7:30	Cooldown – juggling and easy movement.

A few words here about the 'dynamic movements' that are part of the first 10 minutes of practice. Either at the end of that first 10 minute block of time, or interspersed within it, but not at the very beginning of practice, the players should do some vigorous, soccer-like movements. Once they have warmed up a little with the kind of mild exercise that keepaway provides, they can start to make soccer-helpful movements: jogging forwards and backwards, shuffling sideways, walking on their heels, bringing their heels up behind them, alternately, as they run, kicking out straight-legged in front of them, raising their legs, bent at the knee and bringing their legs out from or across their bodies, windmilling their arms around, and shaking out their shoulders. Some may choose to do some traditional static stretching, too. The end, the "cooldown" of practice for the U12's and U14's should include some easy running and some static stretching.

So, for U8 to U14 players, a good way to begin practice is to get everybody <u>on the ball</u>: either in a one ball per player activity or in keepaway. The first part, perhaps a quarter or a third of the practice, is for warming up muscles and minds and competitive instincts, stabilizing techniques, and absorbing a few simple tactical ideas, many of them 'review' from past weeks. In this first part of practice, particular techniques are isolated: picked up from the big game, put over here, off to the side, and practiced intensely. Then the rest of practice is for putting those techniques into context, for applying them, for using them to solve tactical problems; and for learning more about tactics and for improving fitness.

If you consider soccer to be composed of four components (and that's the sensible, traditional way that the United States Soccer Federation presents the game), then you could say that the beginning of practice is technique-intensive and that the rest of practice is an economical (we hope) blend of activities which enhance techniques, tactics, fitness, and mentality.

A Note about the Presentation of These Warmups and Activities
There are three sections under each:

1. "Organization"

This is the set-up, the way the activity is arranged, the form and construction using cones and balls and goals, the conditions of the game. Creating the proper size for each activity is vital, so that the players are motivated and so that they can achieve some technical or tactical objectives. Once you have started a warmup or activity, watch and listen carefully, and be ready to modify the size or dimensions.
Organization should be done briskly and clearly. Talk as little as possible. Get them playing!

2. "Some Benefits"

Always in soccer, the "Why?" is important. We should know why we're using time for this and not for that. The players generally don't ask – they just want to play. Parents may ask, and it's good if we can explain our reasons in an articulate way. Attached to each of these activities are reasons to play them – not an exhaustive list, just some ideas to help you decide how to prioritize using your precious time.

3. "Coaching Points"

There are three rather arbitrary coaching points attached to each activity; there could, of course, be many more. These tips are likely to be useful as the kids play, though, and you can bring them in, one by one, in the same session or over time.

We must remember that the most important thing is that the kids play, practice with the ball, enjoy themselves. If we can enhance their play with some brief, accurate, stimulating pointers, fine. If we're not comfortable 'coaching' – that is, if we would consider ourselves 'activity leaders' and not coaches – no problem. If you're an 'activity leader', just set up these activities, watch, listen, clap your hands, call out encouragement and smile.

If you are a 'coach', these three points may be useful for you to throw out to the whole group, or to demonstrate. If you are an experienced coach or a 'trainer', you can address individual players based on your astute analysis of the player's technical and tactical strengths and short-comings; these coaching points represent the kinds of expressions you would be using.

N.B. Most of these activities are inappropriate for U6's and would be very ambitious for U8's. Those kids can make a whole practice out of the activities in chapter eight. The warm-ups and activities which follow here are intended for U10, U12, and U14 players.

1. Keepaway

<u>Organization</u>: As with many other activities, there are many varia-
tions of keepaway. Let's look at three excellent forms.

1. 3 v 1 in a small rectangle.
("Small" is a fluid term: for a team of U12 girls, perhaps that
means eight by 12 yards. You can start with a grid that size and
adjust it once play begins.) The three passers try to keep the ball
away from the one defender. If one of the passers makes an
obvious mistake – a bad pass or loss of the ball out of bounds,
the player who made the mistake or lost the ball out of bounds
changes places with the defender. If you notice that the defenders are having a really hard time getting the ball, squeeze the
space. If the passers aren't having any success – struggling to
string together five or six passes consistently - make the space
bigger.

2. 3 v 1 in a small rectangle – but this time, play a game "to 3".
The scoring: every time the passers string together five passes,
they score a point. Every time the ball goes out of bounds, or the
defender steals the ball, she or he gets a point. If the ball goes
out of bounds, the passers start a 'new' ball with a pass in from
one of the sidelines. The passers can keep going past five: if
they're really sharp, they can get straight to 15 – and the game is
over! If the defender 'scores', the ball goes back to the passers,
and they start a new count to five. At the end of the game,
change the defender. (One of the passers counts out loud to five
– to motivate the team and to keep track of the passes.)

*3. 4 v 1 or 5 v 1 in a rectangle, with either of those previous
   conditions:*
either the defender and the passer who made a mistake change
roles, OR the group plays a game to three.

<u>Some benefits</u>:

   ◆ Soccer is a simple game: when you have the ball, keep it
      until you can score; when you lose it, get it back before
      those other guys can score! Keepaway provides that
      dynamic tension – keep it versus get it!

- Keepaway is inherently motivating. The passers want to stay passers or to win; the defender wants to get out of the middle or to win.
- Plenty of technique here: passing, receiving, maybe some dribbling and shielding.
- Low key fitness, agility, quickness, concentration.

Coaching points:

- "You don't have to run much, but get out from behind that defender so that the player with the ball can see you and get the ball to you."
- "If you're passing with the inside of your foot, lock your ankle and try to kick the ball with the part of your foot by your ankle – not up by your toes."
- "Keep the ball moving. Bounce it off your foot and keep it rolling – don't stop it. Move the ball – and move yourself with the ball! Don't put the ball in front of you with your receiving touch – play it to the side. That way the defender has to move sideways and space opens up for you to pass through."

2. Free dribbling and turning.

Organization: In an area perhaps 20 yards by 15 yards, all the players are dribbling their balls around freely, trying to avoid bumping into anyone or touching anyone else's ball.
You can make various requests as the players dribble around: that they dribble only with their left or right foot, only with the soles of their feet, that they turn and move off in exactly the opposite direction from where they're going, etc.

Some benefits:

- The most important thing for young players to do is to get good on their feet and with their feet, to gain confidence and stability – and then cleverness and flair – with the ball.
- This activity maximizes ball touches, ball contacts.
- Low key fitness, balance, agility.

- The nervous system is trained constantly: players learn to keep just the right amount of tension in that dribbling foot, to contact the ball exactly <u>there</u> to turn it through 90 degrees, and <u>there</u> to turn it through 180 degrees, to bend their knees, to use their arms for balance.
- One of the fascinations of soccer is simply touching the ball: it's a good idea to give the players one of the things they want most at the beginning of practice.

<u>Coaching points</u>:

- "Hey, slow down a little, stay relaxed – yes, that's good!"
- "Stay up on the front part of your foot – keep your ankles and knees bent and bouncy. Nice and light on your feet, and keep your arms up and out to balance you."
- "Keep changing direction and speed."

3. Quick feet.

<u>Organization</u>:

All the players have a ball. Standing in one place, they play the ball back and forth, from foot to foot, as fast as possible. Then they start to move slowly around the area – moving slowly but keeping their feet going as fast as possible, to play the ball from foot to foot as fast as possible. Ask them to turn often, not to move in a straight line.

You can also ask the players to do this activity in pairs. Two players stand close to one another – two or three yards apart. One plays the ball back and forth between her or his feet and, every several touches, plays it over to her or his partner. That player doesn't stop the ball, but plays it from the receiving foot to the other foot and then continues to play from one foot to the other. Then back to their partner, etc.

<u>Some benefits</u>:

- Maximum ball touches, low key fitness, balance, agility.
- This simple exercise is great for the central nervous system: the players build coordination and quicken their feet.

- In the stage where two of the kids are playing the ball back and forth, they build up coordination and agility and alertness and get in the habit of keeping the ball alive, not stopping it.

<u>Coaching points</u>:

- "Light on your feet! Be ready to play!"
- "Bend your knees!"
- "Come on! Faster with your feet! This is way too slow!" (You say with a smile on your face.)

4. Volleys

Once the ball starts to get up in the air during the game – let's say at U10 – it's good to practice striking the ball when it's off the ground.

<u>Organization</u>:
There are many ways that the players can practice striking the ball when it's up in the air.
Playing with a partner and one ball:

- One player, standing just a yard or two from the other, tosses the ball to his partner, who knocks it back to him with the top of his thigh. Right leg, left leg, etc. The server should toss the ball with two hands, underhanded, for maximum accuracy, and should toss it as rapidly as possible, so that his partner is challenged. After eight or 10 tosses, the players change roles. This activity certainly does not have much 'game usefulness', but it is enjoyable, and it improves timing and balance and coordination.
- Partners stand two or three yards apart, and the server tosses the ball to his partner, who now plays the ball back with the feet, using the inside of the foot or the laces. Right foot, left foot, etc. You can increase the fitness component of this activity in one of two ways. First, as in the previous activity, ask the server to toss the ball to her partner as quickly as possible, so that her partner has to play fast. Second, ask the player who is playing the ball back to the server to run in place – five or six steps, very quickly –

between every toss; here the server does not toss the ball so quickly.

- Next, the toss comes not straight at the partner's body, but off to one side and then the other. Now the player who is volleying has to do 'side volleys', using the laces.
- For more accomplished players, the pairs can do two-touch volleys. When one partner tosses the ball to the other, that player must cushion the ball with the chest, thigh, or foot, and then, before the ball hits the ground, play it back to the server.
- For maximum challenge, have the partners play two touch volleys on the move, back and forth across the field or moving randomly around the penalty area. If the players are sharp and ambitious, and you ask the partners to really challenge one another, this can be a very dynamic end-of-warmup activity.

Some benefits:

- A great activity for balance, agility, and coordination.
- Also, excellent foot-eye training.
- The older the kids are, the more the ball will be in the air.
- Once flying and dropping and bouncing balls become a constant part of the game, it is important to control them as well as all the balls played on the ground.

Coaching points:

- "Up on the balls of your feet now, guys, when you're playing, and keep your feet moving!"
- "Stretch your ankle out – point your toes out straight – and then lock your ankle. Don't let it wobble around. Your knee is what should move, but only a little."
- "For side volleys, turn your body sideways to the ball, then bring your foot around you, with your kicking knee high – and finish with your kicking foot in front of you and on the ground."

5. Juggling

For the youngest players – U6 and U8 – concentrate on ground level soccer: dribbling and ground passing. For older players – those whose games are going to involve flying, bouncing, or dropping balls – give them some time to practice controlling the ball when it is up in the air. Juggling is great to do while waiting for practice to start, after water breaks to focus the mind, or during cooldown. It is also a valuable activity that the players can do on their own or with a friend, in their driveway or backyard, at school recess, on the beach, in a park.

Organization:

All the players have a ball. It is sensible to practice juggling in a progressive way. As the kids master one 'stage', they can move on.
   * As they begin to try to juggle their ball, you can ask them to drop it, let it bounce, and then play it back into their hands. Then they drop it again, etc.
   * Next, they can drop the ball, let it bounce, play it up with one of their feet, let it bounce, play it up, etc.
   * Then, out of their hands and played with their foot – with no bounce – into their hands.
   * Next, out of their hands, played up with their foot – which then hits the ground for balance, and then a second touch with their foot, into their hands.
   * Then, right foot, left foot, without the ball hitting the ground: as many as they can do.
   * Build up to some pattern: right foot, left foot, right thigh, left thigh, right foot, etc.

Juggling with a partner is fun, too:
   * My friend stands close to me and juggles a ball. Every once in a while, she pops the ball over to me. I play it back to her with just one touch of my foot, thigh, head, even chest; she juggles some more and then plays me another ball, etc. Every minute, we change roles.
   * The two of us juggle back and forth, playing two or three touches each. If the ball hits the ground, no problem: we

just flick it up and play on. (But it's a bummer if it hits the ground!)

- ◆ My friend and I work our way down the field and back, playing the ball back and forth, with a bounce in between us, or, as we get better, no bounce.
- ◆ We can try various challenges, too: We each take one touch, then two touches, then three – up to ten; then we work our way down. If we mess up, we start at one again.

Some benefits:

- ◆ Balance, agility, confidence, improved feel for the ball, improved concentration.
- ◆ It's FUN!

Coaching points:

- ◆ "Keep your ankle tensed, but keep your knee relaxed and flexible!"
- ◆ "The higher your foot is when you strike the ball, the more 'soccer-like' your ankle is. If you contact the ball when it's down by the ground, your ankle is sort of L shaped, which is not so realistic in terms of striking the ball with your laces in the real game."
- ◆ "Relax your body – but give the ball your total attention!"

6. One touch passing.

Organization:

There are many ways to do this simple, elemental, valuable activity.

- ◆ Partners stand very close – two to three yards apart – and play the ball back and forth with just one touch: no stopping the ball or setting up the pass with a controlling touch. You can set up challenges to motivate the players: "First pair to get to 20 (each controlled pass being a point) wins!"
- ◆ Partners play the ball back and forth with one touch and continually vary the distance between them by jogging forwards and backwards.

- Partners stand 10 to 15 yards apart. One partner plays the ball as hard as possible to the other; the second partner plays it back softly: both with just one touch. That goes on for 30 seconds – then the players change roles. So the first player is challenged to hit a hard, accurate pass; the second player to play the ball back softly by taking some of the pace off it. This is a great activity to help players learn how to 'weight' a pass.

Some benefits:

- Soccer is a passing game: these activities provide many opportunities to practice striking an accurate pass.
- The partners are playing together, trying to help one another and 'make it easy' for their partner, which is a big component of passing.
- Greatly increased feel for the ball, improved timing and coordination.
- An accurate one touch pass is dangerous and hard to stop!

Coaching Points:

- "For inside of the foot passes: toes up and heel down and hit the ball down by your ankle joint."
- "Aim for the back of the ball, a little bit over the middle line – more at the top half than the bottom half."
- "If you want more speed on the ball: make your foot tighter, use more backswing, and whip your foot through the ball faster."

7. Heading with a partner.

As the Director of Coaching for the California North Youth Soccer Association, Karl Dewazien, astutely says, "If it happens in the game, practice it; if it doesn't happen in the game, don't practice it." Heading is not a feature of U6 and U8 games, so don't practice it with those kids. It begins to come into the U10 game a little, so practice it a little; it's more common in U12 games, so practice it more. At U14 it's an important feature and should be practiced regularly.

These activities are elemental, gentle, meant just as warm-ups or 'introductions'; they are far away from the "finishing off crosses with headers" exercises that your U14's or U16's will do.

Organization:

The players are in pairs.

- My partner and I jog across the field, over and back; we're facing one another, two yards apart. On the way over, one of us, jogging forward, tosses the ball to our partner, who is jogging backwards, to head back into our hands. We switch roles on the way back. Next trip over and back, the ball is tossed to the player jogging forward.
- Facing my partner, who is three yards away from me, I serve three balls, one after the other. The first she heads back to me, strongly, on one bounce: an attacking header. The second she heads as softly as possible, into my hands: a pass. The third she heads forcefully, trying to play the ball right to me, but as high as possible: a defending header. After three rounds, we change roles. Once the players are stable and comfortable doing this on the ground, we can ask them to jump off the ground as they do each of these three headers.
- Two touch headers: standing two or three yards away from my partner, I gently toss her the ball. Instead of heading the ball right back to me, she cushions the ball with her forehead with the first touch, and then, with her second touch, she heads the ball back to me. After 10 or 12 tosses, we change roles.
- 2 v 2 game: pairs playing against each other in a rectangle eight yards wide and 12 to 15 yards long. One pair stands on one of the end lines and, playing as 'goalkeepers', defend their imaginary goal – which is the width of the rectangle and shoulder high. They must stay on the line, but they can move across it. The other pair tosses the ball up and heads it back and forth until they get close enough to try to head the ball into their opponents' 'goal'. If they mis play the ball out of bounds or the ball hits the ground, they must leave the ball and immediately backpedal to become

goalkeepers on their end line; the other two spring off their line, scoop up the ball wherever it hit the ground, toss it up, and begin heading it back and forth, trying to get close enough to the other pair's 'goal' to try to score.

Some benefits:

- Heading is fun. It's also a refined skill that calls for good coordination and timing, which these activities develop.
- These are all 'technique intensive' activities that provide lots of repetition and build up stability and confidence.

Coaching Points:

- "Eyes open wide – watch the ball as long as possible. Close your mouth, though. Strike the ball with your fore head – not the top of your head."
- "Use your whole body: fold your hips forward, drive your shoulders forward, and use your arms for added power."
- "Keep your head steady – brace your neck muscles!"

8. Passing in triangles and squares.

Fast, stable techniques are vital for every player - and passing and receiving are central. If the players in the team can pass accurately and cleverly and receive the ball confidently and skill-fully, they'll be hard to beat.

Often, coaches ask kids at the beginning of a practice to "Get a partner or get into three's and knock a ball around for a few minutes." So the players start moving around randomly, and their passing and receiving are usually vague and careless; there isn't much attention to pace or precision or to the sharpness and excellence of the first touch.

Passing in triangles (or squares) is more demanding and productive. Passes have to be aimed precisely: even though there is no opponent here, the exact line of the pass is important. The pace of the pass will be seen to be vital, too. And receiving must be exact: the first touch must set up the next action smoothly. Asking for the ball, moving at the right moment, and staying alert at all times are important objectives, too.

Organization:

Drop cones down to make triangles of equal sides. Two or three players stand at each cone. At first, the cones can be rather close, maybe 10 to 12 yards apart for a U12 group, then you can expand the sides. The players can do a series of activities:

* "If you're receiving the ball, don't get too close to the cone. Stay back from it two or three yards. Ask for the ball – use your hand and arm and whole body to show that you want it between you and the cone. If you're the passer, play a good, firm pass along the ground between the cone and the receiver so that she can run on to it and be moving when it arrives. Then follow your pass to the next cone.
Receivers: play the ball with the inside of the foot that is 'away' from the triangle, what we'll call the 'front foot', then pass it on with the next touch with that same foot."
* The passes should be crisp and should be delivered about a yard outside the cone; the receiving should be smooth, always re-directing the ball cleanly toward the next cone and quickly setting up the next pass.
* Practice in one direction and then the other.
* When the organization is comfortable and players are making progress with passing and receiving, you can add this request, "If you're about to receive the ball, now try this! As

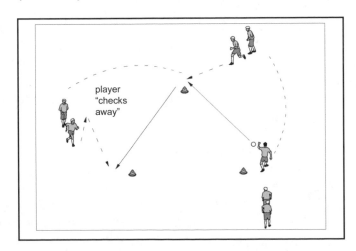

player "checks away"

the ball is arriving to the passer who is going to pass it on to you, take a couple of quick, dynamic steps away from the triangle, jam on the brakes, and come back fast to ask for the ball. Don't do it too soon, or you'll have to stop and stand and wait; don't do it too late, or you'll upset the pass er's rhythm. Come on, be sharp, try to get the timing!"

That stage will reinforce these ideas:
- A receiver using (or 'making') space in which to receive. That is sometimes called "checking off" or "checking away".
- Receivers and passers being in synch.
- Taking a defender, by a short and assertive movement, away from the place where you want to receive the ball.
- "Opening" the game: playing one's first touch at a new, 'open' angle – as opposed to playing the ball back in the direction from which it came ("closing the game").

You can also organize this activity around a square: slightly different angles of 'opening' as the players receive the ball, but essentially the same technical gains and benefits. As the players get more confidence and skill, ask them to play as fast as possible. Game speed, please!

Some benefits:

- This is an intensive technical activity: pass, move, ask for the ball, (or, make space, then ask for the ball), receive, set up the pass, pass, move, etc.
- Precision!
- More ambitious fitness level: this is strenuous.

Coaching points:

- "Strike the ball with a tight ankle – then land on that kicking foot. Make your passing movement be the first step of your run as you follow your pass."
- "Be sharp! Don't be standing still when you receive the ball – be moving in the direction where the ball is going to go.!"
- "At the moment when you're about to receive the ball, get your receiving foot ready. Your other foot (the one that's

going to support your body) should hit the ground just as
the ball hits your receiving foot. Bounce the ball off your
foot (toes up, heel down!), take a stride or two, and make
your pass. Don't let the ball get caught in your feet, under
your body; knock it out in front of you."

9. Turn and shoot.

<u>Organization</u>:

Put cones diagonally in front of a goal – or both goals – as far
away from the goal as you'd like. For the younger players, U8 or
U10, that means perhaps 10 yards from each post, for the older
players, U12 and U14, that means out at the corner of the penalty area. Put another cone out on the field, 10 to 20 yards from
that cone (or from those cones). One player is the goalkeeper,
another goes to the cone diagonally in front of the goal, several
others to the cone out in the field. The shooter starts on the goal
side of the cone nearest the goal, runs around that cone back
toward the passer and asks for the ball. The ball is passed in:
the shooter must receive the ball and then shoot with the second
touch. No third touch allowed! The shooter then goes to the
passers' line; the passer becomes the next shooter. Every eight
or 10 shots, change the keeper.

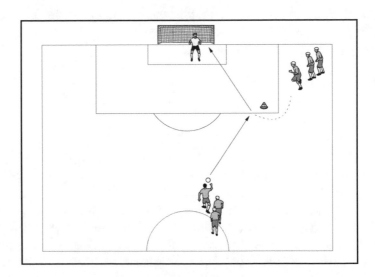

Some benefits:

- Everybody on your team should shoot well. This simple activity is a high-repetition environment where shooters try to outplay goalkeepers.
- The shooters practice asking for the ball, turning with it, adjusting their bodies, and finishing: a vital series of techniques.
- There are multiple technical and tactical objectives here for the passers and the goalkeepers, too.

Coaching points:

- "Passers: play a nice, smooth, rolling ball in, with good pace on it, and aim it to the space towards which the shooter is moving."
- "Shooters, whether you use the inside or outside of your receiving foot, try to play the ball <u>at</u> the goal with your first touch. Not too heavy, or the goalkeeper will take it; not too light, because then you can't stride into the ball and power through it."
- "Shooters, don't just blast the ball! If the keeper doesn't cover the near post, roll the ball into the goal there. If he's off line and doesn't cover the back post, try to play your first touch toward the middle of the goal, 'open the goal up', and beat him to the far post. If the keeper comes out too far, chip it over his head!"

10. Duels in front of the goal.

Organization:

Just like "Turn and shoot", except that now you add a defender. You can put another cone between the shooter's cone and the goal, to the side of it, wherever you want – or you can put a defender in with the shooter and say, "Defend!" However you set up the shooter and defender – next to cones, at each post, at the same post, 'their choice' – the action starts with a 'trigger'. For example, when the shooter moves, or when the passer touches the ball forward to set up the pass which she's going to make with her second touch.

You can challenge the defender by saying: if you manage to win the ball, see if you can pass it back to the next attacker in line. Otherwise, when the ball is clearly not in the attacker's possession, the game is over. When the confrontation is done, the shooters go back to their starting positions, the defenders to theirs. If the shooter misses the goal, she retrieves her ball. Shooters and defenders change cones after a set time.

Some benefits:

- ◆ Players who can outplay their opponents in front of the goal and score are vital to the success of their team. Even at the highest levels, they are rare, so rare that people all over the world know their names: Pele, Hanna Ljungberg, Raul, Mia Hamm, Ruud Van Nistelrooy.

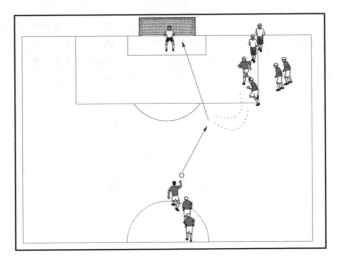

- ◆ Let's get the kids into this crucible early. This activity presents what is perhaps the vital moment in a soccer game: finisher versus defender, close to the goal.
- ◆ The technical stability, tactical savvy, confidence, speed, and toughness of the shooter improve.
- ◆ The concentration, confidence, resourcefulness, and toughness of the defender improve.
- ◆ The passers must be sharp and focused and technically excellent.

Coaching points:

- "Shooters, ask for the ball a little to the side. If the defender doesn't keep up with you, put your first touch into the space in front of you and attack the goal. If the defender over-commits in front of you, jam on the brakes, cut the ball back, and attack the space that she left you."
- "Be strong on your feet, shooters: make yourself wide, use your arms and legs to keep the defender away from the ball."
- "Defenders – be sharp and strong! Watch the ball carefully, keep your balance, and use your legs to get to the ball. If the shooter and the ball get separated, knock it away, or whack him with your shoulder, knock him off balance, and take it!"

11. Driving the ball.

Organization:

Really simple –pairs of players can stand a certain distance apart (20 yards for U10's and U12's, 30 yards for U14's) and drive the ball back and forth to one another. Receive, set it up, drive it, receive, set it up, etc. To add another level of technical complexity: pairs of players face each other at a certain distance. One of the two drives the ball; one of the opposite two receives the ball, in the air if possible, and settles it for her partner, who drives it back with just one touch. You can mark out small squares of cones : these are 'target zones'.

Some benefits:

- Being able to drive the ball hard over the ground or with power through the air is important for crosses, corner kicks, playing 'deep' up the field, switching the point of attack across the field and playing long out of your own end.
- If your players can't play long, accurate passes, your tactical options are extremely limited.
- The essence of virtually every successful team's game is accurate, short-passing possession to build up the attack –

but one incisive, long ball can be a decisive event. Suddenly the ball is out of your midfield and one of your strikers is in on goal!

Coaching points:

- "Stretch your ankle, point your toes down, make your foot tight: now kick through the bottom of the ball."
- "Try to take a fast, dynamic last stride into the ball and follow through strongly. Don't kick the ball – kick through the ball!"
- "Don't overkick! Get up on the ball, get your body moving, then keep your body as composed as possible as you straighten your kicking leg as fast as you can and whip your foot through the ball!"

Chapter Eight

11 Activities and Games for U6 and U8 Players

Here are some important points to remember, for U6 and U8 players, by way of introduction:

- Big words are "FUN", "simplicity", and "patience".
- These activities and challenges are intended to introduce the kids to the ball and to some of the most fundamental aspects of soccer – no more. How does the ball roll, spin, bounce, run away from the dribbler? Everything is new, everything unknown.
- In a simple, understated way, we're starting to train the players' central nervous systems and develop their techniques
- Some of the kids' movements and habits of playing will have only a remote similarity to 'soccer as we know it'.
- These kids are thinking almost entirely about <u>this moment</u> – not last week, not next week, so if we refer to the last game or the future, we probably won't get much of a response.
- There may be – probably will be – a big difference between a child in kindergarten just starting out and a second grader who has played for a couple of years. That second grader is still very young, still just exploring and discovering. However, kids are capable of absorbing and assimilating what they are shown quite quickly, so keep the environment as stimulating and fast-paced and enjoyable as possible.

And there is no reason for us not to be smiling all the time!

1. Dribbling and guiding the ball.

In a small area, ask the kids to move their ball around any way they want, freely. Push it, tap it, kick it along, get the feel of it. Maybe use the bottoms of their shoes, maybe their hands even.

You can pair the kids up and ask one to dribble around and the other to follow her or him closely, dribbling their own ball at the same time.

You can also ask the kids to stop their balls from time to time with various parts of their bodies, as you call them out:
- "Left hand! Good! Now keep dribbling." (Of course, here a certain number may have used their right hand. No problem!)
- " Right foot! Yes, good – and now dribble."
- "Sit on your ball!"
- "Right knee!"

2. Traveling.

With disc cones, make four small squares about two yards on each side, in the four corners of a large square, about 12 to 15 yards on each side. Ask some of the kids to go into each of the four corner areas, and then to dribble their ball from one to the next, all at the same time. They can just go to the next square and stop, or they can go through that one and on to the next, or they can go all the way around – whatever you'd like. Ask them to move in both directions. Then they can dribble into the diagonal square, this time not going around the outside, but through the middle. Ask them to be careful as they all go by one another in the middle!

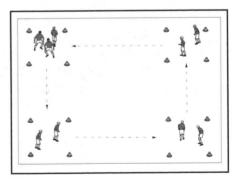

3. Tag.

Tag is an elemental game. There's something primitively appealing about it; it must pull our psyches back to the days when we were hunters.

In a small area, one player holding a pinnie is "it" (or maybe that's you, the leader, just to get things going). When she tags someone else with that pinnie, she hands over the pinnie, and that next player is "it" until she catches someone. If one of the kids is struggling to catch someone else, you can jump into the action, grab the pinnie, and keep the game going.

When the kids get better with the ball, you can also play this way: You, the leader, can move around inside the area, trying to tag kids as they dribble their ball. If you tag them or they lose control of their ball or they dribble out of the area, then they are "frozen" until one of the other kids dribbles by them and tags them. Kids who dribble out of the area can stand on the sideline as they wait to get 'unfrozen'.

4. Dribbling gates.

Over an area perhaps 20 yards square, make lots of "gates" with discs or cones, one yard wide, spread out randomly over the area. Then ask the kids to dribble their ball around the area and to go through as many gates as they can. There are many requests you can make with this simple set-up:
- "See how fast you can dribble through five gates!"
- "I'm going to count to 10. See how many gates you can dribble through in that time."
- "Now, just dribble your ball around at a slower speed. Whenever you come to a gate, push your ball through it, but run around the gate to catch up with it. Here, watch me do it."
- "This time, whenever you come to a gate, push your ball to one side of it or the other, then run through the gate to catch up with it."
- "Run through the gate with your ball, jam on the brakes, come back through the gate the other way, and go quickly to another gate."

- "Now, dribble your ball from gate to gate. Try to dribble really fast through one gate, then slowly through the next, then fast, then slowly...."

5. Relay races.

The kids are in lines of three or four, depending on how many kids are at practice. (Or a line of four and a line of three, which you join to make the lines even.)

Relay races are nice: easy to organize, gently competitive and quick.

Put a cone out 10 or so yards in front of each line and instruct:
- "No ball yet! Just run out around the cone, come back and tag the next person in line. When everybody in the line has done that twice, you're done."
- "Now, each line, please get a ball. The first person in line should dribble the ball out around the cone and back – then step on it when you get to the line. Then the next player takes off with it. Everybody, go three times!"
- "This time, dribble the ball out to the cone, but instead of just turning and coming back, make a complete circle around the cone – here, watch me do it – and then come back. Twice, everybody!"
- "Now, dribble the ball out to the cone and turn around quickly. From the cone, kick the ball back to the next person in line. That person should control the ball and kick it

back out to you. When the ball comes back to you, control it and dribble it back to the starting line. When you step on it there, the next person in line should take off with it. When the last person in line dribbles the ball back in to where you started, you're done!" (This last stage may be ambitious for the five and six year olds.)

6. Kicking at a target.

"Kicking" as opposed to passing – because the kind of intention involved in passing is in the future for most of these kids. But let's get them kicking and striking the ball and beginning to figure out how to make it go straight.

Have the kids pair up, stand about 10 yards apart, and put a marker – a disc or a cone or a pinnie – in front of each of them. Then the two players kick the ball back and forth, trying to hit the target in front of their partner.

After they've kicked back and forth for a while, probably stopping the ball 'dead' each time before they kick, you can say, "Now, every time the ball comes over to you, whether or not it hits the target in front of you, get the ball under control, dribble it around in a little circle, get a look at the target across the way, and have a kick at it."

7. Kicking with movement.

Let's get things moving now:
- ♦ You can challenge the kids with this: you jog around the field and, every once in a while, stop and make a goal by spreading your feet apart. The kids try to dribble along with you and 'score' by kicking the ball through your legs as soon as that 'goal' appears.
- ♦ You can also dribble a ball around and challenge the kids to hit your ball with their ball as often as possible.
- ♦ Then pair the kids up and ask them to try to kick their ball against their partner's ball as often as possible – to keep both balls moving all the time, bouncing one off the other as often as they can. The balls will bounce off one another

erratically and unpredictably, so it doesn't matter necessarily which ball each of the players kicks (although kids at this age can be proprietary: "That's <u>my</u> ball!"), as long as both balls are moving all the time.

8. Shooting.

You can make various challenges:
Set up a course like this – a first cone, a second cone about seven or eight yards from that, and then a small goal about two yards wide, made out of cones, about eight or 10 yards from the second cone. Off to the side about 10 yards, build that same course in the opposite direction.

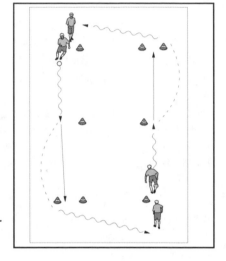

Then ask the kids who are standing at the first cone:
"Dribble your ball ahead, and, before you get to the second cone, try to shoot your ball into the goal. Here, watch how I do it. Then catch up with your ball, come over here, and try to do the same thing going in the other direction. Then come back here where you started and try again! As soon as the player ahead of you shoots, you start."

You can adjust the distances between the first and second cones or between the second cone and the goal – or make the goal bigger or smaller, depending on the kids' ages and how they're doing. Some of the really young ones may even let their ball stop before shooting it: no problem.

For the older kids, you can make the goals a little bigger and ask the kids to rotate through as goalkeepers, just to give them a feel for that position.

9. 2 v 2.

Pair the kids up and have them play little games of 2 v 2 on fields made out of cones perhaps 15 yards wide by 20 yards long (variable dimensions depending on age, skill, and circumstance). The kids can play either 'to lines', where the objective is to dribble the ball over an end line, or 'to goals', where the objective is to score into a goal made out of cones or a pop-up goal or a 'real' small goal. Balls knocked out or hit out of bounds are dribbled back in from the side line (not thrown in); ask the first pair to stand back from the line a couple of yards and let the other pair get the ball in bounds.

There is no great tactical objective here: this is just a visually simple environment where the kids can try to advance the ball or stop its advancement, to gain some balance and athleticism, to get a better feel for soccer, to start getting in the habit of scoring.

Any coaching we do at this stage should be brief and absolutely rudimentary:

- "Look for a nice space of grass and see if you can move the ball there and run around her!"
- "If you can see the goal ahead of you and there's nobody in your way for a moment, shoot the ball in!"
- "If those other guys get hold of the ball, get close to them and get in their way, and see if you can take it back."

10. 3 v 3.

It was stated earlier that a three versus three game could easily, in the beginning years, look more like a one plus two versus three game – as the ball possessor takes on the opposing team and her or his two teammates run along somewhere nearby. In the beginning, it is likely that this kind of moving swarm of small bodies is the reality of a 3 v 3 game.

Progress is generally fast, though, and before you (or the players) know it, there is an even more enjoyable and edifying activity taking place. Here, too, as in 2 v 2, the kids can play either 'to lines' or 'to goals'. In the beginning, especially with five and six year olds, it's probably best to play with no goalkeepers; later you can add them. Then, you can either say that the player nearest the goal is the keeper or you can more formally identify the keeper by putting a different colored t-shirt or pinnie on her or him. Rules are simple, essentially the same as the ones for 2 v 2: no corner kicks, just goal kicks; no throw-ins, just kick-ins or dribble-ins.

3 v 3 is a great game for the U8s; the players are always near the ball (probably way too near in the beginning), so they get lots of contacts, and they're constantly involved in 'soccer situations', like 1 v 1's and 2 v 1's. Here, 1 v 1 is not meant to suggest that rich, tough tactical situation that occurs constantly in the big game: it simply means that two kids who weigh maybe 50 pounds each find themselves face to face. The one with the ball may be thinking, "Wow, I can shoot now!" or "I should run off to her side now and try to get around her....", and the one without the ball may be thinking, "Give me that ball!" That's about all.

This little game will help the kids learn to dribble and to take the ball away, to be more agile and balanced, to stay involved in the action (more or less), and to begin to get a feel for the rich possibilities of soccer. As the months and years click by, the kids will begin to feel the power and efficiency of the triangle: of giving the ball possessor two passing options as well as her or his chances to shoot or dribble – and the strength and solidity of a defensive group of three. The players will begin to absorb intuitively one of the 'geometric realities' upon which soccer is based and which they'll be seeing for the rest of their soccer playing lives.

A very helpful source of information about organizing the 3 v 3 game form is Tony Waiters' and Bobby Howe's Coaching 6, 7, and 8 Year Olds. This book is also a first-rate source of information, in general, about leading and coaching U6 and U8 players.

11. 4 v 4.

For the beginning players, 4 v 4 is fairly close to 3 v 3 in its (relative) visual and tactical simplicity. For older players, there are many subtle or not so subtle visual and tactical differences – but for now the 4 v 4 game is another enjoyable and stimulating activity, and, inherently, another excellent learning environment.

Keep the rules simple here:
- Field is about 40 yards by 25 yards, goal size is flexible.
- No offside. No throw-ins, just kick-ins or dribble-ins. No corner kicks, just goal kicks.
- After a goal, just dribble the ball in or kick it in from the back line. (Leave extra balls behind each goal.)
- As for the flow of play and management, let the players control that.

Keep your remarks simple here, too. At this stage, the players want to be near the action – that is, the ball – and they will be inclined to follow it around the field. Abstractions like "Stay wide!" or "Make some length!" may not have anywhere near the influence of that fascinating, magnetic , rolling ball. So, try to get a few ideas out into the air, and then turn the players loose. Suggest, for example, that when one team wins the ball, they should try to have one player back by their own goal, one player up near the opponent's goal, one player wide on the left, and one player wide on the right. Those players should spread out (which is, of course, an abstraction) to create as much space as possible through which to move the ball (another abstraction!). The team that has lost the ball should try to win it back: the player nearest to it should go after it, and the other three should come a little closer to one another than they were a moment ago and try to protect their goal. Of course, if the ball is with the back player, and the front ('up') player comes back looking for it, don't be surprised: if two – or three! – defenders go charging after the ball, don't be surprised! Just repeat your elemental advice over and over again, patiently, and let the kids feel their way into the principles of the game.

When the players have played this great form for several months – or a couple of years – you can suggest more and expect more. At first, this is a wonderful place for them to learn how to master the ball, to control it under pressure, to figure out how to take it back from increasingly clever opponents. Then, as the years go by, you can help them to learn about situations, likely actions and reactions of teammates and opponents, clever possibilities.

Certainly, we want the players to move along, to advance, to learn. But there is no rush: they need time to feel the game, to stabilize their techniques through plenty of repetition and to dream a little.

By far the best source of information about the possibilities of 4 v 4 is Bert van Lingen's <u>Coaching Soccer</u>, especially the brilliant chapter "4 Against 4: Better Soccer, More Fun!"

Chapter Nine

Activities and Games for U10 to U14 Players

By way of introduction:

- From U10 on, the kids are past the first, exploratory, intro-
  ductory phase – when they are discovering the ball and the
  game, feeling their way into it, getting to know their 'soccer
  bodies' a little. Now comes a vital time for stabilizing their
  techniques, learning the game, and getting into the intentional individual and collective actions and reactions and
  movements of soccer.

- For kids this age, practice organization should be no more
  complicated a proposition than the organization of practices
  for U8's were, but we should now aim to do more with activities that we set up. The most important thing is still for the
  kids to play, and we should trust the activities and games to
  teach them about soccer, but we should use the many
  "teaching moments" that these forms will present to us to
  help the kids along. Our aim now should be to move from
  being an "activity leader" to "soccer teacher" to, as these
  years pass, "soccer coach".

- Now the emphasis should be on polishing techniques and
  using skills in the context of these exciting, stimulating,
  tough activities and games. The overall frame of practice is
  simple: warmup, and, generally, more or less: first activity,
  water, second activity, water and some talk (maybe about a
  set play), scrimmage. During this time, coaches should
  watch and listen, applaud, teach, question, smile, provoke,
  inspire, and enjoy.

- There are many reasons why we should use these activities
  and games – or others like them – as the core of our prac
  tices:
    - Most importantly, they're pure fun.
    - They are easy for us to set up and direct and easy for
      the players to 'read' and understand.

- Because they do not ask players to play a "position", they require and develop problem solving, fantasy, and independent thinking.
- Since they are played in such a small area, they provide many technical repetitions, lots of tactical situations, constant contention, and a vigorous environment where the kids can get fit.
- The players are always around one goal or the other – scoring goals or preventing them; they learn to attack and to defend, to play effectively with and without the ball.
- They're fantastic settings in which to make coaching points, bring out little lessons and show the principles of the game.
- They help the players develop spatial awareness, refine their timing, and become more alert and dynamic; and they call for quick thinking and decisiveness.
- Soccer players have to make some things happen and prevent other things from happening; these games are great environments for developing an active, forceful attitude and approach.

As important as it is to play these small, compressed, intensive games, it is also important to play regular games – 6 v 6, 7 v 7, or 11 v 11 – in 'educational settings', too. That means games where the outcome does not count for anything and you can stop, very occasionally, to make coaching points. Otherwise, the players just get good at playing 2 v 2, 3 v 3, etc. and don't apply all that they've learned in small games to the big game.

As in "Chapter Seven: Warmups and Isolated Games", the activities and games will be presented here in three sections: Organization, Some Benefits, and Coaching Points.

Here are eleven activities or games for U10 to U14 players:

1. 1 v 1.

Organization:

There are at least three ways to set up this essential challenge, this most basic soccer confrontation. Make a rectangle with disc cones, perhaps 12 yards wide and 15 yards long, with "gates" made out of discs three yards away from each end line. These gates are intended to keep the players who are waiting their turn from migrating into the playing area. Three or four attackers, each with a ball, are at one end of the rectangle, behind the gate; three or four defenders are at the other end, behind the gate. As soon as the first attacker enters the rectangle, the first defender springs out from the gate to defend, and the game is on. Here are three ways to organize, and the conditions of the three forms;

1. The challenge is for the attacker to dribble across the opposite end line; there are no goals. If she can beat the defender and dribble across the line, she gives the ball to the defender and goes to the end of the defenders' line. The player who was defending jogs over to the group of attackers. On the other hand, if the defender tackles the ball away from the attacker, she tries to counterattack and dribble over the opposite end line before the original attacker can take the ball back. If she does that, she joins the attacking line; the original attacker jogs over to join the defenders' line.
    Any time the ball goes out of bounds, the game is over. Players keep up a steady rotation: attack, defend, attack, defend, and so forth. As soon as a 'game' ends, the next two players spring into action.

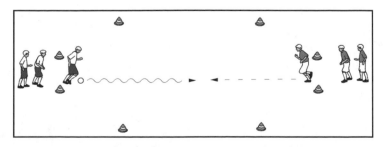

2. Same playing space – but this time make a goal with nine inch cones, four yards wide, at each end. Now the objective is to score a goal. Once the attacker enters the field from the gate, she may shoot at any time; the defender may use her hands, as a goalkeeper, at any time, too. So, for example, if the attacker shoots and the defender catches the ball and immediately rolls it out in front of herself to begin dribbling (as she should), that original attacker can confront her with hands low and try to take the ball away, as a keeper would if a dribbler were breaking in on her. Play goes on until the ball goes into one goal or the other or goes out of bounds.

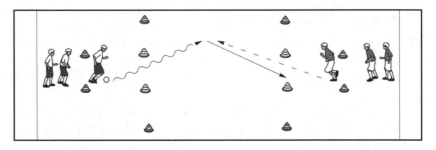

3. Make several rectangles about 12 by 20 yards with goals four yards wide, made with cones, at each end. Pair the kids up and ask two pairs to go to each field. Each pair is a team: a field player and a goalkeeper. The two field players play for a minute against one another, then they become keepers, and the keepers become field players. The players can change on your yell or 'on the fly'. The keepers must stay within three or four yards of their goal, and they can't score. After several minutes, give all the players three or four minutes to juggle or dribble their ball around slowly, to revive themselves: this game is really intense.

Get in the habit of putting extra balls behind each goal. And during these games, concentrate on the scores or the outcomes. If, in the first 'dribbling over the line' game, most of the dribblers are succeeding, move the discs to make the space more narrow, and therefore a bigger challenge for the dribblers. If, in the last game, 1 v 1 plus keepers, there are many goals, shrink the size of the goals. Coaches should always make the environment as challenging as possible.

Some benefits:

- This is the ultimate 'game within the game'. Players must learn to stand on their own two feet, to beat an opponent with the ball and to stop an opponent who is dribbling at them. The visual and tactical simplicity here enhances the learning possibilities.
- There are many technical and tactical remarks we can make here, and the visual simplicity of the form makes analyzing the actions of the players easy for us coaches, too.
- This is also a great game to help the players become dynamic goalkeepers. Not only will all the players have the opportunity to stop shots in the goal, they'll also have the chance to practice their distribution. We certainly don't want the kids to start specializing as keepers at this age, but we should introduce them to the position's fascination and complexity and challenge; that goes for offense as well as defense. It's not uncommon for the player who is playing keeper in the week's game to make a save – and then freeze, with the ball in his hands, gazing out at all those other kids standing there looking back at him, uncertain about what to do. He will often end up tossing the ball randomly out into the field with a motion much like that of a throw-in; the ball doesn't go very far – and it often goes straight to an opponent! In this little game, you can encourage the keeper to move away from his goal once he has possession of the ball; the rules of soccer allow him to hold the ball for six seconds. Then he can try to deliver an accurate pass to one of his teammates by rolling the ball or by dropping it to the ground and then playing it with his feet.

<u>Coaching points</u>:

- To the dribblers: "Run right at the defender, then, just before you think she can reach the ball, push it to the side, accelerate, and either run by her or shoot."
- "Defenders: get out faster, close the distance between the two of you – then move backwards just a little slower than the dribbler is running."
- "If you're playing goalkeeper, stand up with your knees bent and your hands low and in front of you. Don't go down to the ground unless you're sure you can win the ball. Stay on your feet: make the shooter try to beat you!"

2. 2 v 1 plus goalkeeper.

<u>Organization</u>:

Make rectangles about 20 yards by 12 yards, with goals four yards wide on the goal lines. The game: pair the players up and send each of the pairs to a goal. When one of the pairs has the ball, both the players attack the goal at the opposite end, protected by a goalkeeper and a defender. When the two attackers lose the ball – it goes out of bounds, is tackled away or is saved by the keeper – one of them instantly drops back into their goal, and the other stays out on the field to defend. The opponent who was just playing defender and the goalkeeper instantly become attackers. If the ball goes out of bounds anywhere, the 'team' that lost it falls back two yards, and the 'team' in possession dribbles or passes it in.

<u>Some benefits</u>:

- This is a wonderful, visually simple presentation of the common tactical situation 2 v 1. It will present a constant stream of opportunities for two players to try to outplay one – by dribbling cleverly, by shooting, or by using wall passes, through balls, takeovers, or overlaps.
- This is also a great place for those defenders to learn to be clever, tough, and relentless.
- And everybody will have a chance to get into the goal, cut angles, stop shots, start attacks.

154

- "If you have the ball, attack that defender! Run right at him: don't be afraid of him! See how he reacts, what possibilities open up . Can you shoot, can you pass to your friend, can you dribble by him?"
- "If your partner has the ball, stay in the game! Don't 'switch off' and just watch her play: keep scheming and plotting. She needs your help! Can you drag that defender away from your partner, can you make a wall for her, can you sneak in behind that defender and ask for the ball, can you run around and then past your partner (overlap) to confuse the defender?"
- "Remember, everybody: the point of soccer is to score goals. As soon as you win the ball, try to score! Don't hesitate and let the other pair get organized. Always assume that in the next instant you're going to win the ball. Then: how will you score?"

3. 2 v 2.

Organization:

In a rectangle perhaps 15 yards by 20 yards, players can play 2 v 2 the same three ways they played 1 v 1: to end lines, as a dribbling game, to goals, and to goals with keepers in each goal. In that last stage, the two sets of teams and the goalkeepers can rotate, so that the training rhythm for the kids is hard -hard- easy-hard-hard-easy and so forth. If that rhythm is too tough, you can build in a juggling or a one touch passing 'active rest' break. These games are very intense; three or four minutes is a long time. Play – active rest – play – active rest is the way to go. Balls out of bounds are restarted by a kick-in or dribble-in; no corner kicks, only goal kicks.

Some benefits:

- This is another classic 'game within the game' – much more complicated than 1 v 1, and just as vital to master.
- Constant action, many touches on the ball, endless tactical situations and problems, and big fitness.

- This is a particularly good game for developing communication: by words and gestures and body language.

Coaching points:

- "When you have the ball, try to get ahead! Always try to play forward first! If you're under intense pressure, relax, and figure out a way to get away from it – but then, as fast as possible, try to go (shoot or pass or dribble) ahead."
- "When you're defending, stay in contact with your partner. One of you should press the ball! And one of you should work on 'covering' your partner and taking that second opponent out of the game at the same time. That's a big job!"
- If your partner has the ball and he's under pressure, get back behind him at an angle so that he can give you the ball and get out of pressure. If your partner has the ball and he's not under pressure, get ahead of him and ask for the ball. Or, take your defender away from the ball, jam on the brakes, and go back to your partner fast so that he can make a wall pass with you."

4. 5 v 2.

Organization:

Build a rectangle with discs, about 15 by 12 yards, with goals made of nine inch cones at the diagonal corners, on the long sides. The challenge: the five players pass the ball around, trying to keep possession. Every time they string together five passes, they get a goal. The two players try to steal the ball and score into either of those two diagonal goals. The game is 'to three goals' – either three sets of five passes by the five passers or three goals by the 'team' of two. If the passers lose the ball to the defenders or lose it out of bounds, they must start a new string of five passes when they win the ball back or after the two have scored. If they're really sharp, they may make 15 straight passes: that's the game! If the defenders are tough and quick, they'll hustle the passers into mistakes, win the ball, and score three times before the passers can get their passing done: that's the game!

When the ball goes out of bounds, the other team gives the team in possession a couple of yards so that the ball can be dribbled or passed in; then the game is on again. Extra balls are placed outside the rectangle.

The two defenders can easily keep track of their goals. Assign one of the five passers to be the counter – the player responsible for counting, out loud, the team of five's consecutive passes. The coach should never be the counter in such a situation.) Pay careful attention to the scores of these games, too. If the five passers are winning all the games 3 – 0 or 3 – 1, make the space slightly smaller and the goals slightly bigger. If the two are winning the games 3 – 0 or 3 – 1, (and that's surely possible), make the space bigger and the goals smaller.

Some benefits:

- This is a great game for improving the composure and technical sharpness of the passers.
- The defenders will learn to press the ball and cover one another; to hustle, but save energy.
- There are many variations of this game, once you've set up the rectangle and asked the five to try to outplay the two (and vice versa). The two could score goals by other means: by dribbling the ball out of bounds three times or by passing one to the other, once they've won the ball – three times.

<u>Coaching points</u>:

- ♦ "Passers: try to get support for the ball close on the right and left. The other two of you should stay far away from the ball, but look for holes and gaps and spaces where the ball possessor may be able to pass the ball to you."
- ♦ "Passers: don't run so much! Just move intelligently – to support the ball on one side or the other or to stay away – and stay back along the lines to keep the space as big as possible."
- ♦ "Defenders – work together! The first player to the ball should come at it at a slight angle to 'steer' the next pass. If you're the covering defender, don't let the ball go between the two of you – but anticipate that next pass and see if you can pick it off."

5. 3 v 3: attack – defend – rest game.

<u>Organization</u>:

Make a rectangle perhaps 30 yards by 20 yards with goals four yards wide at each end. Make two teams of six, blues and yellows, and then split them in half, so that there are four teams of three players each. One of the blue teams and one of the yellow teams start on the field; the other teams stand behind their goal line. There is a goalkeeper in each goal.

The action: the blue keeper rolls a ball out to one of his teammates, and the first blue team of three starts by attacking the first yellow team. When the ball goes into the yellow goal or out of bounds or when the yellow team clearly gains possession, the first yellow team sprints off the field. If the yellow team now has possession of the ball, they roll it back to their keeper; if the ball has gone out of bounds, the yellow keeper grabs a ball out of his goal. The second yellow team comes on to the field, the yellow keeper rolls them a ball, and they attack the first blue team, who are now defending. When the yellow team scores or loses the ball – for whatever reason – that blue team goes off, and the second blue trio attacks the yellow team that was just attacking. And so forth. First "team" to score five goals wins.

Some benefits:

- This is a dynamic, brisk, challenging game that calls for initiative and fast thinking and concentration.
- The big lesson here is: ball possession is everything!
- When you lose it, you're <u>done</u>: you defend, and you're off!
- This game has a great soccer-like rhythm (play – play – rest – play – play – rest – and so forth) that makes it a fine fitness-building activity.

Coaching points:

- "When you have the ball, try to score as soon as possible! That's the point – and the longer you wait, the more chances there are that you'll lose the ball!"
- "Play fast and try to score – but don't rush. Use your keeper to help you keep the ball and to pull defenders around and change the point of attack. When you have the ball, try to play four against three!"
- "Defenders: stay compact and in touch with one another. Protect the area in front of the goal."

6. 3 v 1 heading game.

Organization:

Make a rectangle with discs, 20 yards by 15 yards, with goals, made out of nine inch cones, eight yards wide, on each end line. One group of three attackers starts with the ball, confronted by a defender and two keepers, who must stay on their goal line, between the cones that indicate their goal.

The action: the team of three tosses the ball up and tries to head the ball back and forth among the three – and to score into the 'goal' at the opposite end, between the cones and below shoulder height of the keepers. If the three score or lose the ball, or the ball hits the gound, one of the three touches a knee to the ground and stays on the field to defend; the other two dash back to their goal line to become keepers. If the ball goes over the goal line, into the goal or not, the opposite team starts back there; if the ball hits the ground, the three (defender and two keepers) sprint out, toss it up, and begin their attack from that point. The scoring: a goal by the attacking team counts as one; a headed ball played over the opposite end line by the defender – at any height – counts as two because you want to motivate that defender to fight and to learn how to clear balls while under pressure.

- This is a logical step up from the 2 v 2 heading game in Chapter Eight: it puts some pressure on the headers. N.B. It's probably best for U10 players to stick with the 2 v 2 heading game; the bigger and more accomplished U12 and U14 players can play this game.
- This game is only moderately strenuous and is a good addition to an otherwise physically demanding practice.
- This game provides practice of three types of headers: sharp, driven headers, hit down at the goal; cushioned, softer headers among the three passers; and strong headers, hit up as defensive headers should be, to clear that opposite end line.

Coaching points:

- "Eyes open! Watch the ball as long as possible! Keep your chin up; use your forehead; don't duck your head."
- "To attack the goal, get over the ball and hit the top half of it. To clear it, get under it and hit the bottom half."
- "If you're fighting an opponent for a header, use your arms for balance and to claim space - and jump first. Then as he jumps, he helps you up."

7. 4 v 2 keepaway – scoring game.

Organization:

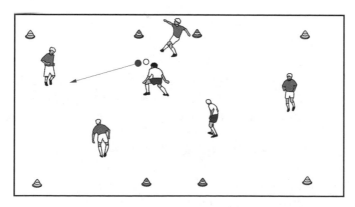

Make a rectangle with discs, about 16 yards by 12 yards, with goals four yards wide, made out of nine inch cones, on the long sides. On one team are two goalkeepers, one in each of the goals, and two wings, who play along the short sides of the rectangle: the challenge for those four players is to string together five consecutive passes. If they do that three times, they win the game. The other team is a pair of 'defenders' who try to take the ball away from the other four and then score three times into either of the small goals – below knee height. If they can do that, they win the game.

Extra balls are behind each goal: any time a ball goes out of bounds – off either team - or any time a goal is scored, one goalkeeper or the other grabs a ball from behind her goal and puts it into play.

After each game ends, the players rotate: goalkeepers become defenders, defenders become wingers, wingers become goalkeepers.

Some benefits:

- This is an intense, multi-faceted game, another compressed environment that will improve technique and offer lots of tactical situations.
- This environment demands simplicity from the players: "Receive and pass, receive and pass" from the four, and "Shoot as soon as you can!" from the defenders.
- Everyone gets a chance to play goalkeeper, to build up the possession, and to score goals.

Coaching points:

- To the wingers: "When the four of you have the ball, stay back along the lines to keep the space big. Glide back and forth along your line to support the keepers when they have the ball."
- To the keepers: "When you four have the ball – stay involved! Come out of the frame of the goal and ask for the ball. But if you lose it, get back into the goal, get your hands down and get coiled!"

- To the defenders: "Keep hustling! Make the four play fast, make them nervous – and if you can win the ball, shoot as quickly as you can."

8. 3 v 1 plus 2 keepers and 3 v 2 plus 1 keeper.

Organization:

Mark out a field with disc cones, 25 yards long by 18 yards wide, with goals eight yards wide at each end. Three players attack a goal defended by two keepers and one defender. If the defender wins the ball, she must play it back to one of the keepers; that gives the other team a moment to organize their defense of two keepers and one defender. If the ball goes out of bounds, it is played back in by a kick in or a dribble in off the sideline by the team in possession. If one of the keepers stops a shot, that team may attack immediately; the other team has to hustle its two keepers back into their goal.

An easy switch, either within a practice or on successive weeks, is to play with three attackers confronting two defenders and one keeper; same essential rules.

Some benefits:

- The 3 v 1 plus 2 keepers is a visually simple situation that gives a big edge to the attackers; it is a forgiving environment for players whose technical skills are not polished.
- Once this form is set up, you can go, in the same training session, from 3 v 1 plus 2 keepers to 3 v 2 plus 1 keeper to 3 v 3 (a full pressured situation!) with no keeper – or with keeper added.
- Three is a big number in soccer: the players should, over the years, gain an appreciation for triangles (as opposed to a line of three players) and the idea of 'third man running' (as opposed to two attackers playing against one defender and the third attacker watching the action).

Coaching points:

- "You three attackers: don't stand in a line. Get the ball to the central player, then the two of you can probe ahead as she stays a little behind you."
- "If the central player gives the ball to one of you 'wings', the other wing should attack the goal.
- "Defender, can you steer the attack to one side or the other by positioning yourself a little to one side of the central player? Then, if she gives the ball to the winger you're sug-gesting, can you get over there and isolate her, and even take the ball?"

9. 3 v 3.

In Chapter Nine, "Activities and Games for U6 and U8 Players", 3 v 3 was recommended as an appropriate game for players of those ages. Here it is recommended again, but with different expectations. With the younger players, 3 v 3 usually amounted to a moving swarm – but no longer. Now the players – U10's to U14's – have different brains and different bodies, more devel-oped perceptions, stronger muscles, and more soccer intelli-gence. They can handle the ball and situations better, and they can make more efficient and calculated actions.

Organization:

Very simple – make a rectangle with discs, perhaps 25 yards by 18 yards, with goals, four yards wide, at each end. No offside, no throw ins; just kick-ins or dribble-ins; no corner kicks, just goal kicks. After a goal, just dribble or pass the ball in. Extra balls are behind both goals.

Some benefits:

- This is another visually simple environment in which many of the essential situations of soccer can emerge: 1 v 1's, 2 v 1's, 1 v 2's, 2 v 2's.
- Constant ball touches, big fitness, all the techniques (except those of the keeper, unless you add keepers), attacking and defending for everybody.

- Again we meet three: an important soccer number. On attack, there is support for the ball and a 'third man running', probing and stretching the defense. The attacking options – shoot, pass, or dribble – are easy to read and put into effect here. On defense, the roles of the three defenders can be highlighted easily:

  1. Defender closest to the ball: press it, get in close to the ball possessor, slow him down, get his head down, hassle him, then take the ball.
  2. Next closest defender: pay attention to ("mark") your immediate opponent, but shade over toward that pressing defender to offer support and defensive strength.
  3. Third defender: don't get drawn in too close to the action. Keep your eye on your immediate opponent but look around, too – imagine where the ball possessor might play a long ball. Try to protect those spaces, away from the ball."

Coaching points:

- "When your team has the ball and one of your teammates is in possession, don't get hypnotized by the ball and stop playing. Stay on the move, try to figure out the best way to make a big problem for the defenders."
- "Always be aware of the two goals, whether your team is attacking or defending. Try to score as soon as you can when you have the ball – and try to speed the game up and threaten your opponent's goal as soon as possible when you've won the ball back."
- "Keep 'doing math' all the time. If you have the ball and you make a 1 v 1 in front of their goal, that's good for you. Attack that defender fast! If you see that you and a teammate have made a 2 v 1, take advantage of it quickly, before the defenders recover. And if you're that one defender, you better call for help fast!"

10. 4 v 4.

4 v 4 is an institution in Holland and is becoming the practice form of choice and even a preferred game form in many other countries.

This is a fantastic game to play - and in which to learn. Everything that youth soccer should include is provided here: an intense, repetitive technical environment, and a simple but compelling tactical setting. By changing the size and shape of the play space, coaches can manipulate the challenges and situations that they want to highlight. For example, if you want to stress the long pass up to the forward, make your rectangle longer and more narrow; if you want to stress switches in the point of attack, make a field that is short and wide and put down goals on each of the end lines, right in the corners. Each team then attacks two goals and defends two goals.

Organization:

For the most basic version of this game form, make a rectangle 35 yards long by 25 yards wide with goals at each end. If you have access to portable gear, you can use 6' by 12' goals or even full size goals, especially if you play with goalkeepers – and you should play with keepers at least part of the time.

You can play either with regular soccer rules or with slightly modified rules: throw-ins or kick-ins, corner kicks or no corner kicks, kickoffs after a goal or just bringing the ball back into play, etc.

Some benefits:

- ◆ The four players in possession can, in a way that three players are unable to do, stretch the field both long and wide; that is, make both depth and width.
- ◆ The feel of this form includes the tactical 'blocks' of players: back defenders, midfield 'support' players, and attacking forwards (as well as keepers if you use them).
- ◆ Players are called on to dominate their immediate opponent

and to control areas of the field in situations that closely approximate those of the 'big game'.

<u>Coaching points</u>:

- To the team with the ball: "Think about when and where to dribble at defenders. If you're the 'up' player, the forward attacker, and you get the ball with only their defender between you and the goal – be ambitious! But if you're the back player, with no teammate between you and your goal, dribble <u>away from</u> that opponent and be very careful."
- "When you lose the ball, think about what the attackers would like to do (shoot, pass up to their forward, make 1 v 1's near your goal, etc.), and fight to keep them from doing that."
- "Come on, talk to one another! Signal, gesture, use your body and the speed and line of your passes to share information and to give messages!"

11. Conditioned games.

<u>Organization</u>:

Let's consider three conditioned game forms that you can set up as alternatives to 'regular' soccer games:

1. Game to one.
Two teams play 5 v 5 on a small field, with a third team of five engaged in some form of active rest: juggling, one touch passing, keepaway, etc. When a team scores, they stay on the field; the team that gave up the goal goes off for active rest; the team that was waiting comes on to play the team that scored. Only goal kicks; kick ins or dribble ins instead of throw ins.

2. Pressing game.
Two teams play 5 v 5 or 6 v 6 or 7 v 7; there is a series of three or four five-minute games. The action: once a team scores, they can not score again: for the duration of the game after their goal, they try only to keep the ball. The other team – which can now use its goalkeeper as a field player and thus has a man advan-

tage – tries to score before time runs out. If they succeed in scoring, the game reverts to its initial condition.
Regular goal kicks and corner kicks and throw-ins.

3. Scoring – passing game.
Two teams play 5 v 5 or 6 v 6 or 7 v 7; the game is 10 minutes long. One team tries, as usual, to score into the opponent's goal; the second team scores a goal by stringing together five (or another chosen number) passes. One of the players on that passing team counts the consecutive passes; another player keeps track of the 'goals'. At half time (after five minutes), the teams change roles.

<u>Some benefits</u>:

- All of these game forms focus the players' minds on a particular intention: they must collectively think together, scheme, plot, help each other to accomplish the special objective that is highlighted.
- There is an exciting urgency to these games that stimulates the players: We have to score! We can't lose the ball! We have to take advantage of our extra player!
- These are good environments in which to coach: they present some classic situations. We can reinforce the necessity to shoot every chance they get, quickly and fearlessly; to spread out the field and polish those shielding skills to keep the ball; to stay on the move and ask for the ball dynamically so that they can keep possession.

<u>Coaching points</u>:

- In the One Goal Game: "Look for long range chances all the time! And you players near the goal: if a teammate cracks a long shot, be sharp: there may be a deflection or a rebound!"
- In the Pressing Game, to the team that is down a goal: "Hey, you're a player up now, so hunt the ball relentlessly! Keep the pressure high – don't let up! If you can get one of their players on the ball to turn his back or if you trap him against a line or in a corner, double him and take the ball!"

- In the scoring – passing game, to the passers: "When you win the ball, spread the field out, stay alert and active, and use your keeper to help you circulate the ball!"

Chapter Ten

11 Ideas About Soccer Fitness

Soccer is beautiful, but it's tough, too. When you play soccer, you breathe hard, you sweat, you bang into other people's shoulders and arms and legs, your legs tangle with other legs as you fight for the ball. Sometimes you get kicked. By the end of the game you're usually very tired.

Fitness is an important component of soccer, particularly when training methods are advancing, kids are playing many months of the year (or are playing other sports), and the game is often taken quite seriously at younger and younger ages.

There are several general points to make about soccer fitness:
- For the kids we are focusing on here, those from U6 to U14, developing fitness is nowhere near as important as developing techniques – although, naturally, we can never absolutely separate technique from fitness.
- For the younger kids – those up through U14 – an active life is most important to build fitness: most of us simply don't have enough time, in one or two practice sessions and a weekly game, to improve fitness dramatically.
- We should never consider overall fitness or the elements of fitness apart from soccer. Later on, at U16 level or in high school or in college, players will be maintaining year-round fitness in a systematic way and will be enhancing their practice sessions with speed and strength training. Our approach should be: with the ball as much possible, in a soccer activity or game as much as possible. As the Dutch say: no running for running's sake.
- Just as we can identify elements of the game of soccer (technique, tactics, fitness, mentality), we can identify elements of soccer fitness. Players must develop agility, balance, speed, quickness, power, cardiovascular and local muscle endurance, and flexibility. As for these elements, if we aim our practices well, we can have quite a dramatic

impact on some of these pieces, like agility and balance. If we're on the right track, we'll also have a positive secondary impact on cardiovascular endurance and flexibility. Most likely we won't have enough time – or the expertise – to influence running speed very much, and we shouldn't be concerned with strength and endurance training yet.

• The best way to get fit for soccer is to play soccer!

Here are eleven ideas about soccer fitness:

1. Soccer is all about agility.

Soccer players must be agile: quick on their feet, able to change direction and speed, control their momentum, swerve, run backwards, shuffle. With and without the ball, they must learn to move their feet lightly but forcefully: one moment softening a foot to control a driven pass, the next instant arranging their feet and their body to fight off the challenge from an opponent, then driving off one leg to unbalance a defender, and quickly pushing off the other leg to go past her.

Some kids are naturally more agile than others; those are the ones we think of as 'well coordinated' or 'naturally athletic'. Everybody needs to get as agile as they can be, though, so we should organize our practices to require as many athletic, dynamic movements as possible.

If our practices include a lot of standing, listening, straight line running, and slow-paced activities, our players will not develop the agility they need. If our practices are an intelligent blend of intense activities and games, active rest, lots of fighting for the ball, and brisk games that demand dynamic quickness, our players will get really good on and with their feet.

2. Balance.

Balance is vital in soccer, too. Players spend a lot of time on one leg: running, receiving, passing, shooting, jumping. Players need time and practice to learn how to adjust their feet and their upper bodies, feel their center of gravity, see how far they can move before they "tip over". This part of fitness is all the more challenging because players are almost always on the move, and they're often trying to maintain or regain their balance while under pressure.

Mostly a question of footwork, balance calls for constant adjustments of the feet and coordination of the rest of the body. Staying on the balls of the feet, flexing the ankles, bending the knees, 'folding' at the waist, and keeping the arms up and out will help. Also critical for balance is keeping the feet under the body. Kids who are stretching out one leg to tackle the ball away from an opponent or who are stretching way out to the side to receive a ball are bound to be off balance. And the kids who stretch their legs out are bound to foul more than those who keep their legs under their bodies.

Think of a surfer who's getting ready to cut back on a wave, all coiled and springy, feet apart, arms out. See her? That's a good model for a soccer player.

3. Starting and stopping.

Soccer is a start-stop, acceleration-deceleration, 'different gears' game. In that sense, it's like basketball, tennis, or lacrosse; it's not like cross country running or long distance bicycling or rowing.

The constant stream of starting and stopping is plain hard work, and the endless changes of pace and of 'gears' require a large expenditure of energy. The more players are engaged in the explosive starts, sudden stops, and varied speeds of the game, the better.

For players up to U14, off-season training is a questionable concept. The kids should just be playing soccer and other sports and staying active. Then, once they begin a soccer season, they should be engaged in practices that approximate soccer games. That means that steady state, straight line running is not relevant.

As much as possible, your practice should provide the players with activities and games where they must start and stop with and without the ball, change speeds constantly, and get used to, physically and psychologically, digging their cleats into the grass, over and over again, to get moving or to change direction.

4. Speed

Soccer speed has multiple dimensions:
* *Speed of thought.* How fast can a player read the game, process information, maybe based on anticipation or intuition as well as on observation, and decide what to do? How fast can a player decide to start moving?
* *Starting speed.* How strongly and quickly can a player get moving and get 'up to speed'? In soccer, the first step is the most important one. Some players are so explosive that their first step gives them a decisive advantage. Think Mia Hamm or Landon Donovan.
* *Technical speed.* How fast can a goalkeeper get down to push aside that low drive that's aimed just inside the post? How fast can a midfielder settle a ball driven at him waist high and play it on to the winger? How fast and stable are all your players when they dribble the ball?
* *Pure speed.* How fast does a player cover ground? If a defender is beaten, can he catch that winger? If the winger gets a step on that defender, can he maintain his advantage and get away from him? On the counterattack, can your guys get forward faster than the other guys can get back?

You can enhance the speed of your players by organizing plenty of activities like tag and relay races, and conditioning your practice games to maximize sprinting. For example, play your traditional 4 v 4 game on a field that is longer and narrower than usual.

As the players are practicing, you can drop in occasional technical points, too: lean forward when you're starting, take smaller steps at first, then lengthen your stride, use your arms – bent at the elbows – to help you accelerate.

Don't worry about 'training' speed. Even with the best methods and plenty of time – much more than most of us have – we would only improve our players' running speed by a few per cent. Technical speed, which we can affect considerably, is much more important.

And what's the point of running faster if you don't know where you're going?

The famous Amsterdam club Ajax, which has a world famous youth development system, considers speed, in all its implications, so important that it is part of their formula for scouting young players. The acronym that Ajax uses to state the essence of the club's philosophy about players is TIPS: Technique, Insight or (soccer) Intelligence, Personality, and Speed. When Ajax scouts are watching young players, they flip the acronym and look first for speed, in all its dimensions, and personality, figuring they can provide the technique and insight through their training methods.

5. Practice should be tough.

This statement does not mean that your practices should be <u>rough</u> or that they should involve inappropriate physical or technical challenges or that your manner should be critical or harsh. It simply means that practices should be as close to the weekly game as possible in their pace and intensity and combativeness.

And while we're considering the notions of "tough" and "challenging", here is an opinion: we should never use physical challenges, like extra running or pushups or sprints, punitively or for motivation. Physical challenges should always be seen in a positive light, should be thought of as stimulating and desirable. Running or activities like pushups or situps should never be used to punish a player for using bad language or a team for being a little flat or for losing a game.

Too many practices are soft and sluggish, with too little physical and technical challenge. Then on Saturday, the game is fast, vigorous and contentious. The difference between Wednesday night's practice and the Saturday game is so great that the players feel as though they're in two different worlds – and we're left wondering how they can look so good on Wednesday and so shaky on Saturday.

Practice environments should be fast, demanding, filled with duels and struggles: tough. Part of the fun of practice is fighting for the ball, trying to dominate, trying to outplay the opponent, trying to win.

Let's say I'm on a U12 team. I come to practice at five of six on Thursday night and right away get into a keepaway game. That goes on until 6:10, then we practice turning with the ball and other footwork until 6:20, with some dynamic stretching movements interspersed. After a water break, we play 2 v 2 line soccer until 6:45, then we get into 1 v 1 duels in front of the goal, until 7:00. After another water break and a short 'paragraph' from our coach about defending corner kicks (two reminders), we play 7 v 7, then have a nice cooldown.

Whew! That's a lot of running, pushing on the ground, jamming on the brakes, bumping into people, scoring, tackling, scrapping. Got kicked a couple of times, knocked over once. I'm tired. I feel great.

6. As much as possible with the ball.

The ball is fascinating, magnetic, motivating: it's fun to dribble it, shoot it, head it, catch it.

The ball should be central to almost everything we ask the players to do. During the game, it dominates the players' attention and largely dictates how they move – with it and without it. Activities and games which include the ball are more enjoyable and stimulating and realistic. If you have set up some tough games with the ball, the kids tend to forget about the hard running, the exertion, the 'training' component. Without the ball, there is just 'training'.

7. Playing other sports.

Playing sports other than soccer is a good idea. Some sports are more similar to soccer than others in terms of fitness, of course, but involvement in virtually any other sport will enhance soccer fitness. For example, if kids play basketball or tennis, their footwork and cardiovascular fitness will almost surely improve; lacrosse and hockey players get stronger and tougher, too.

As much as kids love soccer, it's not a bad idea for them to get away from it for brief periods from time to time, too, as they engage in other sports. They'll come back to soccer fresh and eager and motivated, and most likely, in excellent shape.

8. Pre-season training.

For U8 to U14 coaches, pre-season training is not relevant for their teams. It is included as a topic here only because youth coaches should engage themselves in the whole spectrum of soccer in their communities, from U6 to high school. For the great majority of players, high school soccer is the last time they will play 'formal' soccer, so the high school game could be considered the culmination of all the players' practice and involvement in the game.

If youth coaches are interested in their efforts having a proper end – and that end is the constant enjoyment and improvement of their players – then they will be attentive to the quality of soccer coaching in thier high schools. With all due respect to all those many good-hearted high school soccer coaches, often the quality of high school coaching is not what it should be. And one aspect of high school soccer that is consistently questionable is pre-season fitness training.

Let's say that a coach has 10 pre-season training sessions with his players: twice a day practices for five days. Not uncommonly, the team runs in the morning – long distance runs, sprints, shuttles – often without a ball. Then the team practices in the afternoon: techniques, tactics, and set plays. These sessions, particularly the afternoon ones, can go on for hours. The morning running sessions are, to be blunt, a waste of a lot of valuable time.

Here are a few suggestions for high school coaches:

- Ask your players to do their cardiovascular preparation, to build their fitness base, during the summer. Say to them: we're not going to do any long distance running once we're back together as a team.
- Don't try to get your team "fit" in that first week. That's unrealistic, unhealthy, and undesirable. You can't possibly get kids fit in a week; you'll only overload and exhaust and possibly injure them, and you want them to be most fit and as fresh as possible later in the season. Start slowly and gently, emphasizing dynamic stretching before and static stretching after every session.
- Whenever it's possible, use a ball in training. Shuttle runs, relays, small sided games: always with a ball.
- Do not train for more than 90 minutes at any time. Two 90 minute sessions – three hours – is more than enough for a pre-season day, physically and psychologically. Here, less in more.
- Organize your sessions precisely: concentrate on technical improvement and tactical savvy – and, by intelligent pacing and by alternating easy physical activities with demanding ones, build fitness.
- Keep in mind the start-stop, heartbeat up-heartbeat down, walk-jog-run-sprint quality of soccer and approximate that quality in all your pre-season activities.

Some high school players refer to pre-season as "Hell Week": that's truly unfortunate. The first week of preparation for the coming season should be wonderful: filled with enjoyment and learning, as well as a certain amount of hard work and discomfort, for sure.

The suggestion that youth soccer coaches should scrutinize the quality of high school coaching – particularly fitness preparation – is not made lightly. It is not intended to advocate meddling or interfering in the high school coach's program, either. But if we expect our years of efforts to have a productive ending, we may have to have a difficult (and diplomatic and respectful) talk with our local high school coach or athletic director.

If our town's players end up enjoying high school soccer as much as possible and playing the kind of skillful, elegant, intelligent game we should expect of 15 to 18 year olds, such a difficult talk will have been worth it.

9. Rest.

We are a fast paced society, busy seven days a week. Everyone seems to be on the move all the time, dynamic and diligent; the notion of 'doing nothing' is way out of favor. We don't just work hard and keep moving: we multi-task. The relentless pace of life is accepted as normal, even as a challenge. Who can do the most, work the hardest, be most committed?

The world of youth sports has been affected (afflicted?) by this cultural reality. Kids play lots of sports, seasons blur into one another, seasons pile up on top of one another. Healthy, enjoyable, athletic activity, all during the year, is good – but constant, formal, scheduled training and practices are questionable. When a 16 year old girl is coming to a two hour off-season soccer practice in a gym, on a Saturday in February, after an hour long pre-season lacrosse practice and then going off to an evening hockey game (as happened recently in suburban Boston), it's past time to draw the line.

As coaches, we should regard the issue of rest just as attentively as we cultivate the players' motivations to play hard. We should talk with the players (this is mostly for U12's and U14's, not U8's and U10's) about getting enough sleep – at least eight hours, every night, resting their bodies as much as possible one day a week, and taking it easy on practice and game days. We should also talk with parents about the dangers of over-scheduling: it's easy for kids to get involved in a 'seven days of activity' lifestyle: school Monday to Friday, one practice Tuesday, another practice Thursday, one game Saturday, another game

Sunday. For kids, especially those hitting growth spurts, that could be quite a tax. As well, if the kids are going seven days a week, the <u>family</u> gets no rest.

10. On being "athletic".

We often hear how "athletic" certain soccer players are. At tryouts, one coach will say to another, "Yes, he's really athletic." It has been said that our women's national team has been dominant for so long because we have so many 'athletic' players.

Generally this term means 'coordinated', 'fast', 'strong': that bundle of physical talents that help an individual to be an able athlete. There is no question that good soccer players are well coordinated, strong, and fast, but when we're dealing with young (U8 to U14) players, we should keep priorities in mind. It's impossible to overstate this idea: the most important consideration for young players is to get good with and on their feet, to train the central nervous system, to become precise and cultured in controlling the ball. That means that we should narrow the meaning of 'athletic' for younger players, focus it, particularize it. Athletic with the ball: fine. Devoted to strength and speed training: no.

For many reasons, coaches can become enticed by fitness and athleticism, by the desire to build up their team's strength and force. Culturally, we Americans are pre-occupied with fitness and the athletic look, so the feeling that coaches should always be improving their team's athletic aspect is always in the air. Coaches may feel that a lack of strength and speed is what keeps their team from reaching that next level. Many new coaches, who may lack confidence about their ability to teach soccer but who have an athletic background, figure that they can effectively help their kids get stronger and faster and tougher. Some coaches like to have specialized fitness gear, like speed ladders, around.

For U8 to U14 players, though, the best way to become more athletic is to play soccer. Later, at the U16 or high school level, after puberty, kids can do special strength and endurance training. For now, get better with the ball, learn the way the game goes, ***PLAY SOCCER!***

11. Priorities

Some elements of youth soccer coaching bear repeating. Here's one: for U8 to U14 players, technical training is most important, followed by tactical learning, followed by fitness preparation. Of course, each affects the others, and we can never absolutely isolate one from the others. When we're planning our training sessions, though, technical advancement should be our primary objective.

The primacy of technical improvement puts some particular burdens on coaches. We must learn about techniques and methods of coaching so that we can most effectively help our players to improve. We must organize our practice time well so that our players have the greatest number of technical repetitions and plenty of tactical situations. And we must construct our training sessions so that relevant fitness opportunities are maximized.

11 Practice Sessions

This chapter provides descriptions of eleven hypothetical practice sessions. There are imaginary – but realistic – practices here for U6 through U14 players; the accounts of the practices include technical and tactical pointers, practical suggestions, and responses to situations.

These descriptions are intended to show how age appropriate practices are put together, how they flow, how we can intervene and have influence, how we can manage time, how much is enough for the time allotted. The sessions are described from the point of view of the coach (the "I").

Practice lengths are from 45 to 90 minutes, hypothetically, in the evening, between 6:00 and 7:30 P.M., although U6 practices often take place just before the week's game.

U6 Practice Session One

6:00 to 6:15

Free dribbling, footwork, relays.

I was here at 5:45 to look over the field, get my gear organized, and set up cones for the activities to come. One of the spaces I set up was a 10 by 15 yard "Dribbling Zone" – kids who arrived early could go in there and dribble their ball around if they felt like it. At 6:00 I asked all the kids to come inside that space and, after I greeted them all and asked them how they were doing:

- "OK, come on, let's move around in here with our ball."
- "Good, that's it – push it along with your foot."
- "Try to dribble in different directions all the time – not in a straight line."

Then they did a couple of minutes of footwork, knocking the ball back and forth between their feet, standing still and moving slowly around. "Be nice and bouncy on your feet, everybody! That's it!"

After a few minutes of free dribbling, I asked them, rapidly:

- ◆ "Stop your ball with one of your hands! OK, good, now dribble some more."
- ◆ "Stop your ball with one of your feet."
- ◆ "Quick! Turn and go the other way! Do that again! And again!"
- ◆ "Sit on your ball!"

Then some relays. There were eight kids at practice; I joined them and made three groups of three. I put three nine inch cones out eight yards from a line and organized a group in front of each cone. Then we:

- ◆ Ran out around the cone, without the ball, came back, and tagged the next player. The first group of three to get everybody out and back twice was the winner.
- ◆ Next, we did that with a ball: the first player dribbled out and around the cone, came back, and stepped on the ball. The second player took it out and around – and so forth. When everybody had made two trips: done!
- ◆ Then out and, instead of just turning around the cone and returning, dribbling all the way around the cone, in a circle, and then coming back. Two trips each.

6:15 to 6:25

Kicking at a target (Game Six in Chapter Eight). I asked the kids to pair up quickly. Then: "Each of you please stand behind one of these cones. (I had put down pairs of cones, eight yards apart.) Get a ball and kick it back and forth: try to hit your partner's cone. If your partner hits the cone in front of you, stand it up, and kick the ball back at his cone. Come on, now – try to hit that cone over by your partner every time!"

I just let the kids kick away for several minutes. After a while I said, "OK, now, guys, if you and your partner knock over one or the other of your two cones three times, give me a yell." At 6:25, we took a break for water.

6:30 to 6:45

Before practice, I made two small fields, 20 yards long and 15 yards wide, with goals made out of cones, four yards wide, at each end. After the water break, I made new pairings, and the boys played two 2 v 2 games, side by side, for 10 minutes. No formality: if the ball went out or into a goal, the other pair just dribbled or kicked it back in: game on. I stayed off to the side; I didn't interrupt the game at all.

- "Great shot, Cleo!"
- "That's the way to do it, Frank!"

After that, we took a break, drank some water, and got organized for our weekly game.

U6 Practice Session Two

6:00 to 6:10

Before practice I made four small squares of cones, two yards on each side; these small areas were the corners of a larger square, 15 yards on each side (the "Traveling" game from Chapter Eight). Then:

- "OK, girls, just dribble your ball into the next square, in this direction (I pointed to each of the 'next' squares) and stop."
- "Good – now go the other way, this way, and, instead of stopping in the next square, dribble into it but keep going to the next square. Watch how I do it."
- "Now, turn around again – and dribble through all the squares until you're back to where you are right now."
- "That was excellent! Now go all the way around in the opposite direction."
- "Now turn around so that you're going this way – that's right – and let's see which pair of you is first to get back to the square where you are right now. Go!"

6:10 to 6:20

I quickly rearranged the cones, and we spent 10 minutes playing "Dribbling Gates" (Game Four in Chapter Eight), the girls dribbling their ball from gate to gate with various conditions.

6:20 to 6:25   Water and relaxing.

6:25 to 6:40

We finished with a free 3 v 3 game on a field 25 yards long and 15 yards wide. Since there were eight girls at practice, each side had one sub; I rotated them in every two minutes, so the girls would play for six minutes and rest for two.
- "Come on, girls: score a lot of goals!"
- "Yes, Julia, that's a great shot!"
- "That's the way to do it: move up the field toward the other goal!" I said that, but I know that if they're tired, they might rather stand still; and that, in any case, where they're most likely to run is where the ball is.

At 6:40 I told the girls that I was really proud of them – and that I had enjoyed our practice tonight.

U8 Practice Session One

As usual, I arrived a few minutes early to check the field, set up, and get myself organized. As the players arrived, I greeted them and said hello to their parents. Then at six o'clock:

6:00 to 6:15

I asked the girls to dribble their ball around freely inside a 10 by 12 yard rectangle I had built with cones.
- "Keep changing direction, girls!"
- "Use only the insides of your feet."
- And a minute later: "Now just the outsides."
- "Now, on your own, every several touches, turn all the way around with your ball and dribble away in exactly the opposite direction. Use both feet to turn the ball."
- "Move the ball around using only the bottoms of your shoes, only with the cleats."

186

We finished up this part of practice with a game of tag, this way:

- ◆ "Now, girls, dribble your ball around inside this same area. If I tag you with this pinnie I'm carrying, you're frozen. You have to stop, pick up your ball, and make a goal with your feet apart. If somebody else comes along and passes their ball between your feet, you may dribble again. If you run out of bounds to get away from me, you're frozen with one foot on the sideline. You know me: I'm lightning fast! I'll bet I can freeze all nine of you!"

After about 40 seconds (a long time for me!), I passed on the pinnie to Jennifer, took her ball, and she was it for 30 seconds. Then she gave the pinnie to Alisha.

6:15 to 6:25
We played 1 v 1 in a small rectangle with goals four yards wide at each end.
"See if you can get a little to the side of the defender, girls, and shoot the ball past the defender into the goal!"

6:25 to 6:30 Water and some conversation.

6:30 to 6:45
I joined the group of nine players, to make a total of 10. Then on two small fields, we played a game of 2 v 2 and a game of 3 v 3. Every several minutes, I joined a different team and reconfigured the teams.

6:45 to 7:00
After a quick drink of water and just enough time for me to move the cones to make a bigger field (to one about 35 yards long by 25 yards wide), we played a game of 4 v 4 plus goalkeepers (5 v 5). After every goal, a new keeper ran into the goal for both teams, and we took a moment to change our positions within the team (up – back – right – left) before we restarted.

U8 Practice Session Two

The boys started practice with some footwork: knocking the ball back and forth between their feet, first standing still and then moving slowly around the 10 by 15 yard area I'd built with cones. They moved slowly, but I asked them to keep their feet going as fast as possible. "Touch the ball as often as you can! Come on: faster!" Then the 10 boys paired up and did some footwork exercises together:

- "Knock the ball back and forth between your feet six or eight times, then play it over to your partner – who should be standing about three yards from you. When it comes to you, don't stop it: play it from one foot to the other and then start knocking it back and forth between your feet. Take six or eight touches and knock it back to your partner. Quick!"
- "Now play the ball back and forth between you – but use only one touch this time. Just bounce the ball back and forth. Aim for the top curve of the ball, and keep your ankle tight!"

6:10 to 6:20

Then we moved to another area where I had set up discs for Dribbling Gates (Game Four in Chapter Eight). I asked the boys:

- "Push your ball through a gate, run through after it, and go to another one. Keep moving from gate to gate."
- "Now push your ball through the gate, run around the gate, catch up to your ball, and go to another gate, then others."
- "Now when you get to a gate, dribble your ball through, stop, spin, and come back through the other way."
- "Next, when you get to a gate, dribble your ball through, but go around one disc or the other and come through the gate again, in that same direction. Here, watch me do it."
- "Last – get together with a partner and keep one ball with you. Dribble your ball to a gate and make three passes through it. Then your partner dribbles to a gate, and the two of you make three passes before you dribble off to the next gate – and so on."

6:20 to 6:25 Water and some talk.

6:25 to 6:40

The 10 boys played a game of 3 v 3 line soccer in a small rectangle and a game of 2 v 2 in a small rectangle. Both games were "line soccer": the object was not to score a goal, but to dribble the ball, under control, over the opponents' end line. If one team got across the other line, they left the ball, and the other team (pair) immediately came back the other way. If the ball went out of bounds, over any line, the team that lost it fell back a couple of yards, and the team that now had it dribbled it or passed it back in. A couple of times during this 15 minutes, I changed the teams.

6:40 to 7:00

A free game of 4 v 4 plus goalkeepers (5 v 5) on a field 35 yards by 25 yards with six foot by 12 foot goals (which our town has plenty of) at either end. I didn't coach here today: I just called out encouragement from time to time.

U10 Practice Session One

The usual pre-practice routine: check the field, set out the cones, organize gear, check my 3 x 5 card to get my coaching brain warmed up.

As the kids arrived, I greeted them and waved to or spoke to their parents, and I got them going on 'shooting and saving'. In pairs, six or eight yards apart: one, a 'keeper', rolled the ball to the other, a 'shooter', who shot it back at her with one touch. Nice firm, low shot, but not too hard. The keeper scooped it up or caught it and rolled it back. After 10 or 12 shots, the players changed roles. (By the end of the season, I want to be asking the shooter to hit knee high or waist high – and for the shooter to be able to do that.) No technical pointers to the 'shooters' or the 'keepers' here: I just wanted them to start warming up, to start soccering. Then, at six o'clock:

6:00 to 6:10

      There were 10 girls at practice tonight, so we started with games of 4 v 1 keepaway in rectangles that I had made with discs, 10 yards by 12 yards. Simple: the four tried to maintain possession; the one tried to force the four into making an error or take the ball. If the four lost the ball out of bounds or to the defender – by a bad pass or bad reception – the player who made the mistake changed with the defender.

      I asked the four girls who were passing the ball to stay out of the corners: to stay back along the middle of the sidelines and 'cruise' back and forth along those lines to support one another. "If the ball is with the player next to you, come toward her, but be sure to stay back against your line: that gives her support, but keeps the field big, too. If the ball is with the player across from you, resist the temptation to come into the field! Stay back against your line and keep the field big! The ball will probably be with one of the players to one side of you or the other in a moment – or it may come flying over to you!"

      And to the player in the middle, I kept saying, "Keep hustling! Make them play fast! Force them to make a mistake!"

6:10 to 6:25
Turn and shoot. (Game Nine in Chapter Seven).
      I split the 10 girls up into two groups and sent five to each goal. There, one of them jumped in to become goalkeeper for eight or 10 shots; the other four rotated, as fast as possible, between passing and shooting.
      I stressed precision: "Come on, girls! If you're passing, give your friend the kind of pass you'd like to get: rolling flat and fast – but not too fast. And shooters: don't try to overpower the ball! Once you've turned the ball toward the goal, get your balance and hit a nice, firm shot just inside one post or the other."

6:25 to 6:35
Water and some talk about throw-ins. I went over the technical points. "Let's be sure that every throw-in is legal. A throw-in is a pass, so let's treat it like every other pass. Throw the ball at your teammate's foot, with some speed, but not too fast."

6:35 to 6:50

At the end of the break, I made a rectangle of cones, with goals at each end; then we played 3 v 1 plus two goalkeepers (Game Eight in Chapter Nine). I asked the two "spare" players, one on each team, to stand behind the goals and juggle or dribble a ball and to change 'on the fly' from time to time. Today I stressed finishing: "Be sure that every time you have the ball you produce a threatening shot!"

6:55 to 7:15

After a quick changeover to get organized, the girls played a 5 v 5 game: four plus a keeper on each team. After every goal, the teams changed their keeper.

I didn't coach much here: just reminders, or coming on to the field to make a picture about shooting.

The 3 x 5 card in my pocket tonight looked like this:

Pre	Shooting and saving
6 – 6:10	4 v 1
6:10 – 6:25	Turn and shoot
	Good pass!
	Accuracy over powering
	Shooting!
6:25 – 6:35	Water
	Throw-ins
6:35 – 6:50	3 v 1 + gk
6:55 – 7:15	5 v 5

U10 Practice Session Two

6:00 to 6:20

At the very start of practice, I told the boys how proud of them I was last Saturday: that I thought that everyone had played well, especially the three who had shared time playing goalkeeper. "I really liked the game because it was so loud: you guys are communicating very well. Keep that up: it's important to share information and to encourage one another!"

Then all the players began to dribble their ball around, freely, inside a 12 by 15 yard area I had built with cones. After two minutes I said, every minute or so:

- ◆ "Right foot only."
- ◆ "Now left."
- ◆ "Now move your ball only with the bottom of your shoe, with your cleats. Stay light on your feet: be creative!"
- ◆ "Next: as you dribble, from time to time, make a complete circle with the ball around your body and then go on in the direction you were going before. Hey – don't make a circle around the ball with your body: make a circle around your body with the ball! Use the insides and outsides of your feet to turn the ball – and use both feet."

After they had done that for about a minute, I said

- ◆ "Good! But now move faster! Bend your knees more as you turn! Imagine that there is an opponent trying to take the ball away from you."
- ◆ "Now, dribble the ball at an angle, a little to the side, with the inside of one of your feet. Every couple of touches, bring that dribbling foot around behind the ball and use the outside of your foot to burst off in the other direction. Then dribble at an angle with your other foot and do the same thing. Keep making zigzag lines like that."
- ◆ "Now for a minute: dribble any way you want to: be creative!"

Then I came into the 12 by 15 yard area with a ball and a pinnie.

- ◆ "OK, boys, I'm it. If I tag you with this pinnie, I'll hand it to you: you're it. I have to be dribbling my ball when I tag you. If you leave your ball as I'm chasing you – or if you dribble out of bounds – you're it. Here we go!"

6:20 to 6:35

In a rectangle 15 yards long and 12 yards wide with goals four yards wide at each end (and with "gates" made of cones, two yards behind each goal), the boys played 1 v 1 this way: an attacker came through the gate on to the field and could shoot at any time. The condition: shots had to roll through the goal on the ground. As soon as the attacker went through his gate, the

192

defender could go through his gate: the defender could tackle the ball away or, if he wanted to, he could use his hands at any time, like a goalkeeper. If the defender tackled the ball away or stopped a shot with his hands or took the ball off the dribbler's foot as a keeper might, he could counterattack to the opposite goal. Some of the boys just 'played defense', but many of them played 'as a keeper' when they confronted the attacker. Play went on until the ball was through one goal or the other or out of bounds. After each game, the players changed lines.

There were many quick games here: an attacker would rush out and shoot quickly, missing the goal entirely. End of game. But there were some fantastic games, too. The best:

Ben dribbled out, moved a little to the side, and shot. Rodney, who had come toward him quickly, got his hands on the ball and scooped it up. Then he dropped it in front of him and dribbled at Ben, who tackled the ball away from him, and, as it bounced to the side, got down low and grabbed it with his hands. He quickly tossed it to the side and shot it – and Rodney somehow flashed his hand out and knocked it out of bounds. Everybody was cheering!

6:35 to 6:45
Water and some talk about how we're going to attack on corner kicks. I brought the boys over to one of the goals and showed them this organization:
   ♦ The wing on the side where the ball went out takes the kick.
   ♦ The other wing goes right in front of the goal to threaten it.
   ♦ The center forward stands between them and back a little, away from the goal: the three forwards make a sort of flat triangle.
   ♦ The back on the side of the ball moves up aggressively.
   ♦ The other back comes over to the middle of the field, at an angle to and behind the other back who has pushed up.
   ♦ The goalkeeper should be about a third of the way up the field.

"Now if you're the winger taking the kick, look at the picture and decide what to do!"

6:45 to 7:15

There were 11 boys at practice, so I joined them, and we had a 6 v 6 game to finish: two 12 minute halves and a four minute half time. I stopped the game four times, arbitrarily, two at each end, and asked the attacking team to take two corner kicks, one on each side: we fine tuned each one.

After practice tonight, Henry's father asked me if he could speak with me for a moment. Henry is a very good player, eager, outgoing, clearly loves the game. He often comes to practice in a Manchester United shirt; I'll bet that he has soccer posters up on his bedroom wall. His father said: I think Henry should get more playing time during games: he's really into soccer, and he's probably (and the father said 'Please excuse me for saying this') the best player on the team. Some of the other kids are clearly not as good or as into the game.

I thanked the father for being direct, and I said this: I appreciate Henry's liking soccer so much, and I, too, think that he's a really good player. I'm already giving him the most time in games that I can – a few minutes 'extra' here and there. And at this level, in this situation, that's all I will do. I owe it to all the kids – except for changes due to disciplinary issues – to give them equal playing time: not 'to the second', but as close as I can make it. I simply can't see the future, and all the kids should play the same amount now.

I suggested that the father should try to figure out how to get Henry involved in some pickup games in their neighborhood, and we talked about the local club and camp scene. I could tell that he was not particularly satisfied with our conversation, but we said good night cordially.

194

U10 or U12 World Cup Night

In one of the two U10 or U12 practices each week, or, alternatively, using one of every two U10 or U12 practices, I organize a World Cup. This is how:

From 6:00 until 6:15, the team does footwork (Quick Feet or various turns or a highlighted dribbling move) and plays tag; we build in a little dynamic movement and stretching, too. Then from 6:15 to 6:25, the kids play 3 v 1 keepaway or 4 v 1 keep-away in small rectangles. Very simple: make a mistake and you're in the middle.

At 6:25, everyone drinks water, and we get organized into teams of three or four – depending on how many kids are at practice tonight.

Here is how the last practice went: (U10 boys' team: 12 players at practice, so we played 3 v 3 games, no keepers, on fields 30 yards long by 20 yards wide, with small goals made out of cones). Rules are simple: no corner kicks, only goal kicks. No throw-ins, just kick-ins from the sideline. After a goal, just bring the ball into play from you end line, by dribbling or passing. Referee your own game. All free kicks after a foul are direct.

6:30 to 6:40
>Tunisia 3 – Denmark 4
>Japan 4 – Brazil 3

I made up a 'scoreboard' on a 3 x 5 card ahead of time and filled it in right after each game. After the first game I got the players together and talked to them about the front attacker, the 'up' or 'deep' player: how important it is for that player to stay close to the opponent's goal and stretch the length of the field and how important it is to receive passes with his body turned sideways, ready to roll off or spin off the defender. I made a picture of that, too.

6:45 to 6:55

> Tunisia 4 – Brazil 5
> Japan 4 – Denmark 3

After that game, I gathered the players and reminded them about how important it is to stay wide and low and balanced when going into a tackle – and I demonstrated that.

7:00 to 7:10

> Brazil 3 – Denmark 3
> Japan 2 – Tunisia 3

After a quick congratulations to Japan, we played a free game of 5 v 5 plus keepers (6 v 6) on a field 50 yards long and 35 yards wide, for 10 minutes, had a cooldown, and talked for a few minutes.

U12 Practice Session One

6:00 to 6:10

As the girls arrived, we had one, then two keepaway circles. At 6:00, when everyone had arrived, we had two small circles of 6 v 1 keepaway. The conditions: if you make a mistake, you're in the middle; and if you move backward, to get away from the defender in the middle (or if you force someone else to move backward because you gave them a bad pass), you're in. Moving side to side a little is no problem; as a matter of fact, that's good.

I kept encouraging the girls to get up on the balls of their feet, to stay calm, and to move fast.

6:10 to 6:25

There were 14 girls at practice tonight, so I sent seven to each goal, and we played "Duels in Front of the Goal" (Activity Ten in Chapter Seven). I stressed to the girls that they should try to use the defender's pressure against her: if she over-committed to one side or the other, to play the ball into the space created via a roll or spin with the ball, and take their shot.

6:25 to 6:35

Water and some talk about defending throw-ins. "Get yourself goal side and ball side of your closest opponent and get ready! Someone should mark the thrower. And don't forget that there's no offside on a throw-in!"

6:35 to 6:55

We played the 4 v 2 keepaway – scoring game (Game Seven in Chapter Nine). As 12 of the girls played those games, I kept my eyes on them as well as I could from a distance, and I took aside the two girls who play most of the time in the goal for us and helped them with their footwork and catching technique. A couple of times, after I'd gotten the two of them going on a repetitive activity, I'd jog over to the two 4 v 2 games and offer a reminder or shout out some words of encouragement.

6:55 to 7:25

After a few minutes to move cones and get teams organized, we finished with a 7 v 7 game: two 10 minute halves and a five minute halftime.

This game format gave me an opportunity to 'practice', too. During the first half, I watched the game carefully, so that at halftime I would have one piece of advice for each team. Then at halftime I 'practiced' by telling the blue team to shoot more quickly and the yellow team to stretch the field better, long and wide, in as effective a way as possible (and the girls 'practiced' listening to me!). Then in the second half I observed the action carefully to see if my words had any impact.

7:25 to 7:30

We cooled down with a little easy running, some juggling, and some stretching.

U12 Practice Session Two

6:00 to 6:20

We started practice with 20 minutes of individual footwork: free dribbling, turning through 180 degrees, moving the ball with the bottoms of the feet, a couple of feints, and moving the ball around the body with the insides and outsides of the feet. We started slowly, threw in some dynamic stretching movements as we went along, and finished at a high, demanding pace.

6:20 to 6:35

3 v 1 keepaway in a small rectangle. There were 15 boys at practice, so I jumped in to be the 16th, and I kept changing the groups so that I spent a few minutes in each of the rectangles.

6:35 to 6:45

Water and some talk about attacking the opponent's goal when we knew that a cross was coming. We went to one of the goals and made a picture with three players running as the crosser moved down the sideline: one to the near post, fast and straight; one to the far post, bending his run and coming in later; and one drifting into the 'hole' behind those other two attackers, setting up around the penalty spot.

6:45 to 7:05

I stayed in the mix as the 16th player and separated the team into four groups of four. Then we played 1 v 1 plus goalkeepers (the third form of Game One in Chapter 10) in four small rectangles with goals at each end. We played three minute games, the attacker and goalkeeper for each team changing freely; then I would gather everyone for a minute or two to make a coaching point ("Lower and wider on your feet when you defend – and don't lunge for the ball!", "Keepers, the closer the shooter gets, the lower your hands should be!")

7:05 to 7:25

Then, from the group of 15 boys, I made three teams of five. I asked each team to organize themselves (at least for the start of the game) in a GK – 1 – 2 – 1 system, then I put two teams on the field, asking the third team to go off the field and practice juggling or, in pairs, one touch passing. Then we played one goal games (the first form of Game 11 in Chapter 10) on a small field 30 yards long and 25 yards wide with goals six yards wide made out of cones at each end. Goals had to be hit below knee height. Score and you stayed on; the other team scored, and you went off for 'active rest', and that third team came on to play.

I didn't coach much in this stage, other than to keep encouraging the boys to put hard pressure on the ball when they were defending.

U14 Practice Session One

At the beginning of practice I told the girls that I was very happy with how they had played the previous Saturday, even though we had lost our game 3 – 2. "That team was as good as we were – maybe better, maybe not – but I thought that we controlled the game most of the time. That last goal that they got from the corner kick was a great header, and that was about the difference in the game. The way you passed the ball and communicated and helped one another and the smarts that you showed – those things were all excellent. OK, let's have a great practice tonight!"

6:00 to 6:15
- ◆ "Dribble your ball around the center circle. Do what you want: be creative."
- ◆ "Now dribble some zigzag lines with the insides and outsides of your feet."
- ◆ "Juggle your ball."
- ◆ "Now get together with a partner and keep one ball up in the air. Neither of you should touch it more than three times in a row before you pass it over to your partner."
- ◆ "Quick, now, get into a group of three and keep the ball up. Same condition: three touch maximum."
- ◆ "Now juggle your own ball with your feet only."

- "Good! Now do some dynamic movements: shuffle diagonally, bring your knees up behind you to touch your hands, swing your feet up high in front of you – you know how it goes."

6:10 to 6:25

We now did some passing: I put down two triangles of cones, 12 yards on each side, and split the 16 girls into two groups; two or three players went to each cone. Then the girls played two touch passes around the cones – and followed their passes to the next cone. They:
- Moving counter-clockwise, received the ball with the inside of the right foot and passed on with the next touch of that foot. "Make your passing motion the first step of your run!"
- Same, in the other direction, with the left foot.
- Moving counter-clockwise, received the ball with the outside of their right foot, played it across their body with that touch, and passed it on with the inside of the right foot.
- Same, in the other direction, with the left foot.
- Moving clockwise, received the ball with the inside of the right foot, played across their body with that touch, and passed it on with the outside of the right foot
- Same, in the other direction, with the left foot.

Since our town has the kids passing around triangles from the age of nine on, these girls are really getting sharp. I kept up a stream of technical reminders, and, for sure, demands, to keep them on the upbeat.
- "Tighter ankle, Molly!"
- "Hit the top curve of the ball, Rachel!"
- "Two touches only, Katya! Three is too many!"

6:25 to 6:35

Water and some conversation about playing with a back line of three. We've been playing 3 – 4 – 3, so I had some questions for the girls about a few game situations. I used discs, on the ground next to the bench, to draw out those situations as we drank water and stretched a little.

6:35 to 6:55

Now we pulled one of the goals up so that it was about 45 yards from the other one. I asked the team's primary two keepers to go into one goal or the other. Then I split the remaining 14 girls into two groups. One went off to the side to play 5 v 2 (Game Four of Chapter Nine) on a field that I had marked out with cones.

The other seven girls went to the right side of one goal (as it faced the field) or the other – three at one goal, four at the other, each with a ball. The first two girls at each goal made eye contact, pushed their ball out in front of them, and played a diagonal ball to the other girl. Then they received the pass coming their way, turned as quickly as possible, and, with their second touch, shot the ball at the goal from which they had just come.

They retrieved their ball from the goal, or the keeper rolled it out to them, or they chased after a miss ("If you miss, you must run after your ball – no jogging!"), and then they went back to the post and got ready for their next turn.

- "Careful with that first touch, girls! Get the ball – and yourself – around quickly!"
- "Bend your knees and use your arms to help you get balanced."
- "Concentrate on the target! Try to put the ball just inside the post – or OFF the inside of the post!"

After 10 minutes, the two groups (the 5 v 2 group and the shooting group) changed places.

7:00 to 7:25

After a quick drink of water, we organized an 8 v 8 game, both teams playing GK – 2 – 3 – 2. Tonight, as we often do, we scored the game this way (with gratitude to the Swedish Soccer Association): a goal shot into the net counted as one, a ball off either post or the crossbar counted as two, and a goal off either post of the crossbar counted as three.

7:25 to 7:30

Cooldown was some easy running and stretching.

U14 Practice Session Two

Typically, some of the boys arrive a few minutes early for practice; several came early today. For those who felt like it, I had a game of circle keepaway going: a small circle, only a few yards in diameter, around a player in the middle. "Make a mistake and you're in!"

Then at 6:00 o'clock, after a few words of welcome, I got the boys going with several simple technical activities:

6:00 to 6:20
I asked the boys:
- "Dribble your ball around in this half of the penalty area, guys, please. Lots of touches, lots of changes of direction. Slow down, not so fast!"
- "Now, for a couple of minutes, turn with your ball every several touches, and go in exactly the opposite direction. Nice and light on your feet!"
- "Dribble only with the outsides of your feet, now."
- "Now do some dynamic movement: get your knees up and open up your hips, walk on your heels, or do some easy high kicks – you know about it."
- "Juggle your ball now: only feet, no thighs."
- "Now juggle with a partner: three touch maximum and then give it to your partner."
- "Now keep juggling with your partner – but each of you now should take exactly two touches when the ball comes to you."
- "Good, good! Now head the ball back and forth with your partner."
- "Do some more dynamic movements for a minute now."
- "Get together with a new partner, please. Stand about three yards away from him and play one touch passes back and forth. Try to play as fast as you can!"
- "Now, for the last two minutes, move around this half of the field with your partner and play driven passes in the air to one another. Don't let the ball hit the ground as it comes to you. Control it in the air, settle it, dribble it a few touches, and play an accurate ball that your partner can take out of the air."

6:20 to 6:30

The boys played passes around two triangles of cones. I urged them to play the ball fast, to use their kicking motion as the first step of their run to the next cone, and to ask for the ball dynamically and with lively body language.

6:30 to 6:40

Water and some conversation about our last game. We played a very aggressive, physical team last Saturday; they had two players in particular who went in hard, and on several occasions, knocked our players over. The boys had been upset at halftime; they felt that the referee was not calling the game tightly enough, and one of our boys had even suggested retaliation. I told them at the time that that was out of the question - that anyone who retaliated or got into any kind of verbal altercation would be taken out immediately – but I also told them to look out for themselves. I didn't have the sense that the other team was dirty or cynical – just too wound up.

Now I told the boys that I was proud of them for playing well on Saturday and for avoiding dumb fouls and payback. I repeated my conviction that we owe the game respect, but I told the boys not to be naïve, to be sharp and clever out there, to expect some rough treatment along the way. We had a short conversation: most of them were nodding in agreement as it finished – although a couple looked skeptical and one looked as if he thought I was naïve. So be it. The game must be played in the right spirit – even by wound up adolescents.

6:40 to 7:05

We had a 2 v 2 plus keepers tournament. Since there were 15 boys at practice, here's how I organized it:

I made five teams of three players each. Four of those teams started two games on two fields 25 yards long and 15 yards wide, with goals six yards wide at each end. I asked the teams to rotate the keeper and the field players as they wished. The fifth team was off to the side, juggling. Rules: no corner kicks, only goal kicks; kick-ins or dribble-ins, no throw-ins. Extra balls were behind each goal.

Games were three minutes long, followed by two-minute breaks. During the breaks, I made a coaching point or 'painted a picture'.

- ◆ "Defenders, one of you must press the ball, and the other should figure out how to help your partner - and, at the same time, play your immediate opponent out of the game."
- ◆ "Keepers, when you have the ball, make a good pass to one of your teammates. You must not lose the ball back by your goal!"
- ◆ "Hey! If your partner has the ball, and there's no pressure on him, move ahead! If there is pressure on him, come back at an angle behind him or maybe try to do a takeover with him."

Then the teams rotated to a new opponent, one went off, and the team that had been juggling came on.

7:05 to 7:25

We organized quickly into two teams and played a 20 minute 8 v 8 game (I joined the boys as the 16th player). We brought the goals up to the top of each penalty area and played with the usual field width.

I stopped the game several times to point out situations where there was not enough pressure on the ball or where cover was poor (too close to or too far away from the pressuring defender or at a bad angle – so that the covering defender would not be able to step up and prevent danger if the pressuring defender lost his grip on the ball possessor.

7:25 to 7:30

Cooldown was some easy running, static stretching, and last remarks.

Appendix

In this Appendix are reviews of 11 books or sets of books and 11 videos/dvds or sets of videos/dvds. There are certainly other excellent and helpful books and other inspiring tapes on the market. The number 11 here is simply in keeping with other sections of the book.

These reviews are intended to clarify and inform, for coaches or organizations that would like to build up their libraries. They can be considered recommendations. The order here is random; these are not rankings.

Books

Teambuilding: The Road to Success, *by Rinus Michels*

Rinus Michels, the author of this book and FIFA's "Coach of the Century", is the most astute, inspirational soccer philosopher of all time. This is a comprehensive, ambitious book, filled with theoretical insights and practical ideas: a reflection of a lifetime of deep thinking about soccer and human beings.

Coaching Soccer, *by Bert van Lingen*

This is a definitive book, a genuine masterpiece, indispensable. Bert van Lingen is an extraordinary thinker and long-time colleague of Rinus Michel's; he has written here a coherent vision of how soccer players meet soccer, how they play – and how coaches coach. This book is loaded with wisdom and practical help. The chapters on 4 v 4 and "Soccer Training" are particularly compelling.

Especially for anyone who is fascinated by the flair and superb play of the Dutch (who isn't?), Coaching Soccer will be inspiring and edifying. There are enough stimulating ideas and suggestions here to occupy a coach for years.

Basic Training and **Advanced Training** and **The Complete Goalkeeper**
> *From Success in Soccer* (www.successinsoccer.com)
> Basic Training is aimed at U6 to U14 players and their coaches; Advanced Training is for adolescent and high level amateur players. These two books are translations of material from the German Soccer Federation: impeccable, superbly organized and produced, with lots of philosophy and a fantastic collection of games and activities. The goalkeeper book combines first rate technical pointers, excellent photographs, and a comprehensive collection of activities for developing young goalkeepers.

Principles of Team Play, **Systems of Play**, and **Modern Tactical Development**
> Three short theoretical books from *Allen Wade*. These are direct and straightforward, clear explanations of various tactical ideas: concepts like depth in defense and attack, principles for organizing your team, and movements with and without the ball. These meticulous but down to earth books are excellent for coaches who are moving up to the 11-a-side game.

The Coaching Philosophies of Louis van Gaal and the Ajax Coaches
> This book offers a look into the philosophies and methods of one of the world's most famous clubs -which also happens to have a world-renowned youth development system. Great chapters on their youth program and on goalkeeping.

Conditioning for Soccer, *by Raymond Verheijen*
> A high level, ambitious book: unless you are coaching U12 players at minimum, this book may not be for you. But if you're leading older players, this is an indispensable resource from which to gain information and ideas about the fitness aspect of soccer.

Developing Soccer Players the Dutch Way,
by Henny Kormelink and Tjeu Seeverens
Lots of good insights about age-appropriate objectives and activities; a fine overview of youth progression, especially for clubs trying to compose a coherent program.

The **FUNdamental Soccer** series, *from Karl Dewazien*
Four books (Practice of Champions, Tactics, Goalkeeping, and Guide) filled with simple, down to earth, accessible ideas and activities. These books are excellent for beginning coaches: comprehensive, helpful, practical.

The **Coaching** series, *from Tony Waiters (some co-authored with Bobby Howe).*
Four great books, progressively designed for players of various ages. Coaching 6, 7, and 8 Year Olds and Coaching 9, 10, and 11 Year Olds are more practical than theoretical: great resources for dynamic, enjoyable practice activities; easy to read; and accessible to coaches without a lot of experience. And if you're a more experienced coach, you'll admire the clear organization and positive tone, as well as the activities' resource. Coaching the Player and Coaching the Team are for leaders of older kids: U12's and U14's. They are more theoretical, more abstract, designed for 11-a-side soccer.

Any or all of: **Offensive Soccer Tactics**, **Defensive Soccer Tactics**, or **Soccer Systems and Strategies**, by Jens Bangsbo and Birger Peitersen
These are ambitious, high level books for experienced, soccer-savvy coaches of at least U12 and U14 teams. They all include plenty of theory, clear and cogent ideas, and a multitude of helpful – but high level! – activities for your practices.

Brilliant Orange: The Neurotic Genius of Dutch Football,
by David Winner

If you want to read a whimsical meditation on the conjunction of culture and sport, and an admiring tribute to one of the world's greatest soccer nations and its singular collection of stars, this is the book for you. You'll never think about soccer (or politics or architecture or decision making!) the same way after you've read it. When you order your copy from your local bookstore, encourage the owner to stock extras!

Videos/DVDs

The Dutch 4 v 4 Training Method

The Dutch refined and formalized the 4 v 4 game form as a teaching tool, and they use it as a basis for instruction. This tape highlights teaching points, particularly technical ones, and includes lots of game footage of kids playing and enjoying 4 v 4. American soccer would be improved dramatically and radically if more practice sessions for U10 to U14 players looked like the action on this tape.

Coaching Under 9's

The famous Dutch player and coach Johan Neeskens is highlighted here, working with groups of young kids. The desired simplicity and enjoyment of good youth practice sessions shine through on this tape.

Individual Defending

This is an excellent source of ideas about how to present defending concepts, how to teach young players how to play when the other team has the ball. Many coaches don't so much teach defending as they rely on their team's combativeness; this tape offers plenty of teaching points.

Success in Soccer: various tapes

There is now an impressive array of tapes available from the Success in Soccer company, all of them superb. These tapes cover everything from dribbling moves to juggling to "Ball Oriented Defense". For the players who are the focus of this book, particularly helpful are <u>Fun and Games, Volumes 1 and 2</u>: fantastic looks at practice environments, filled with great images and practical ideas; and <u>Advanced Technique Training, Volumes 3 and 4</u>, more ambitious stuff for the U12 and U14 players.

Coerver videos

The Dutchman Wiel Coerver and his training methods are world famous. These tapes incorporate a wide array of dribbling moves; combinations; and fast-paced, repetitive technical activities. The <u>Coerver Fundamentals</u> tapes (a set of three) precede the more recent <u>A New Era</u> set of three. Every one of these six tapes is clear and comprehensive; the production is highly professional and first rate.

The material on these tapes is ambitious and deep. There are fantastic clips of world stars showing their skills, and the youth players who model some of the activities are precocious: their demonstrations are elegant and beautiful. Just about all the activities on the tapes are relevant for – or could be modified for – inclusion in U10 or U12 or U14 practices, but the presentation here is ambitious, particularly for beginning coaches. For coaches with background and experience, they are a first-rate resource of teaching inspiration and skill-building activities.

From International Tactics, five tapes: **Individual Attacking**, **Individual Defending**, **Group Attacking**, **Group Defending**, and **Methods of Training**.

Brilliant is the only possible word for these unique tapes. Composed by Jape Shattuck, a world class soccer thinker who has been men's soccer coach at Harvard, Director of Coaching for the Massachusetts Youth Soccer Association, and an instructor for both the United States Soccer Federation and the National Soccer Coaches Association of America, these five tapes are a visual encyclopedia of soccer knowledge. They combine impeccable organization and scripting; beautiful footage of World Cup action; and comprehensive, precise coaching pointers. If you want to learn the 'stuff' of soccer coaching, there is no better source.

2002 FIFA World Cup: All the Goals
It's good to have a highlight tape or two around, and this is a great one. 161 goals recorded from different angles, many with buildup moves, many taped in slow motion. This tape makes clear the power, precision, and phenomenal skills of the best players in the world.

For the players this book is intended for – U6 to U14 – goalkeeping is not a main priority. But because U12 and U14 players need guidance in the fundamentals and because most youth coaches do not have much experience with and therefore confidence in teaching goalkeepers, there are four tapes or sets of tapes about goalkeeping recommended here.

The Soccer Goalkeeper, *with Frans Hoek*
A superb, progressive, comprehensive group of three tapes: thorough and excellent teaching pointers with impeccable examples of repetitive technical activities and a solid treatment of tactical activities, like the pass to the keeper. Frans Hoek has been an assistant coach and keeper expert at Ajax and Barcelona, and with the Dutch national team; these tapes feature inspiring footage from Ajax training sessions.

Dutch Goalkeepeing Drills, Volume Two: Advanced Skills
This is high level stuff, only for accomplished keepers of U14 level – and perhaps some advanced and ambitious U12 kids. The activities are presented clearly, with excellent examples by experienced keepers; this is a source of many technical-ly-intensive activities, not so much a 'pick up some teaching pointers' resource.

Keeper, *by Tony Waiters* (Two tapes)

Clear, coherent, progressive principles and teaching points and practice routines, delivered with a deft touch and down to earth style by the former England keeper and extraordinary teacher Tony Waiters.

Goalkeeping: The DiCicco Method (Three tapes)

Tony DiCicco, former women's national team coach, makes goalkeeper training clear and accessible; these are engaging, superbly produced tapes. Tony also shows here (as do Frans Hoek and Tony Waiters) how vital high energy and a trustworthy, positive connection to the players are.

About the Author

Dean Conway has been a teacher
and soccer coach for over 30 years
and is now an instructor for the
United States Soccer Federation. He
was the State Coach and Director of
Coaching for the Massachusetts
Youth Soccer Association from 1992
until 2003.